Reduced Instruction Set Computer Architectures for VLSI

ACM Doctoral Dissertation Awards

1982

Area-Efficient VLSI Computation
by Charles Eric Leiserson

1983

Generating Language-Based Environments
by Thomas W. Reps

1984

Reduced Instruction Set Computer Architectures for VLSI
by Manolis G. H. Katevenis

Reduced Instruction Set

Computer Architectures for VLSI

Manolis G. H. Katevenis

The MIT Press
Cambridge, Massachusetts
London, England

Publisher's Note

This format is intended to reduce the cost of publishing certain works in book form and to shorten the gap between editorial preparation and final publication. Detailed editing and composition have been avoided by photographing the text of this book directly from the author's prepared copy.

Second printing, 1986

This dissertation was submitted in October 1983 to the Department of Electrical Engineering and Computer Science, University of California at Berkeley, in partial fulfillment of the requirements for the degree of Doctor of Philosophy. The thesis research was sponsored in part by an IBM Graduate Student Fellowship and by the Defense Advanced Research Projects Agency (DOD) ARPA Order No. 3803 and monitored by NESC under contract #N00039-78-G-0013-0004.

This book was typeset by the author in *troff* and printed on a Postscript™ printer made available by Adobe Systems, Inc. Printed and bound in the United States of America.

Library of Congress Cataloging in Publication Data

Katevenis, Manolis G. H.
 Reduced instruction set computer architectures for VLSI.

 (ACM doctoral dissertation award; 1984)
 Originally presented as author's thesis (Ph.D.)—University of California, Berkeley, 1983.
 Bibliography: p.
 Includes index.
 1. Computer architecture. 2. Integrated circuits—Very large scale integration. I. Title. II. Series.
QA76.9.A73K37   1985   621.3819'5835   85-78
ISBN 0-262-11103-9

Αφιερώνεται
στους Γονείς μου,
που μ' έμαθαν να χρησιμοποιώ
λογική και τάξη στο να λύνω τα προβλήματα,
κι αγάπη γιά τον Άνθρωπο στο να τα διαλέγω.

*Dedicated
to my Parents,
who taught me to use
logic and order for solving problems,
and love for People in choosing problems to work on.*

Contents

Series Foreword

Each year the Association for Computing Machinery (ACM) conducts a world-wide competition to select the best doctoral disertation. The only restriction is that the dissertation be written in English. A cash award of $1,000 is given to the author by ACM, and the winning dissertation is published by The MIT Press with appropriate royalties. The award is presented annually at the Computer Science Conference of the ACM.

The ACM has appointed a selection committee with members from academia and industry. This year the committee reviewed twenty-one dissertations and chose the thesis "Reduced Instruction Set Computer Architecture for VLSI" by Manolis G. H. Katevenis as the winner. The thesis work was supervised by Professor Carlo H. Séquin, University of California–Berkeley. The selection committee was composed of L. V. Dowdy, N. V. Findler, Robert R. Korfhage, and John R. White, with James Gray of Tandem Computers serving as chairman.

Dr. Katevenis's thesis was judged to be an outstanding contribution in the debate over computer architecture. A long-standing issue is, should one build a simple machine in the style of Seymour Cray's CDC 6000 series and the more recent IBM 801 and RIDGE machine or should one build a machine that directly supports a higher-level language, such as Bob Barton's Burroughs 5000 series and the more recent IBM system 38 and Intel APX432. Historically the arguments have focused on performance and usability. Katevenis's thesis is that the introduction of VLSI adds a new issue to this debate: how to spend the real estate on a single chip processor. He argues that a simple architecture allows the CPU to fit entirely on a single chip and even allows space for pipelining the processor and caching data from primary memory. In addition, he argues that it is easier to write good optimizing compilers for a simple machine.

This thesis explains the concepts of a Reduced Instruction Set Computer (RISC): a computer that has a simple and uniform instruction set. It demonstrates the thesis by showing an implementation of a particular RISC machine and comparing it to other designs, notably the Motorola 68000 and the DEC VAX. Along the way the thesis provides a charming narrative of the design decisions that went into the RISC II project, its achievements and mistakes. It stands as one of the best tutorials on the issues of VLSI processor design.

Charles L. Bradshaw
Chairman, Awards Committee, ACM

Preface

Integrated circuits offer compact and low-cost implementation of digital systems, and provide performance gains through the high bandwidth of *on*-chip communication. When this technology is used to build a general-purpose von Neumann processor, it is desirable to integrate as much functionality as possible on a single chip, so as to minimize *off*-chip communication. Even in Very Large Scale Integrated (VLSI) circuits, however, the transistors available on the limited chip area constitute a scarce resource when used for the implementation of a complete processor or computer, and thus, they have to be used effectively. This dissertation shows that the recent trend in computer architecture towards instruction sets of increasing complexity leads to inefficient use of those scarce resources. We investigate the alternative: Reduced Instruction Set Computer (RISC) Architectures, which dedicate the chip resources to supporting only the most frequent activities — simple instructions, and fast access to frequently used operands.

In this dissertation, the nature of general-purpose computations is studied, showing the simplicity of the operations usually performed and the high frequency of operand accesses, many of which are made to the few local scalar variables of procedures. Then, the architecture of the RISC I and II processors is presented. These feature simple instructions and a large multi-window register file, whose overlapping windows are used for holding the arguments and local scalar variables of the most recently activated procedures. In the framework of the RISC project, which has been a large team effort for more than three years at the University of California, Berkeley, a RISC II nMOS single-chip processor was implemented by this author, in collaboration with Robert Sherburne. Its microarchitecture is described and evaluated, followed by a discussion of the debugging and testing methods used. Future VLSI technology will allow the integration of larger systems on a single chip. The effective utilization of the additional transistors is considered, and it is proposed that they should be used in implementing specially organized instruction fetch-and-sequence units, and data caches.

The architectural study and evaluation of RISC II, as well as its design, layout, and testing after fabrication, have shown the viability and the advantages of the RISC approach. The RISC II single-chip processor looks different from other popular commercial processors: even though it has less total transistors, even though it spends only 10% of the chip area for control rather than one half to two thirds, and even though it required about five times less design and lay-out effort to get chips that work correctly and at speed on first silicon, it executes integer, compiled, high level language programs significantly faster than these other processors made in similar technologies.

Acknowledgments

It was only through a coordinated team effort that the Berkeley RISC project evolved from a concept to the reality of silicon chips and a C compiler. I would like to deeply thank all those collaborators who contributed to this effort, some of whom are mentioned in § 1.2.

In particular, I would like to thank three of them. Carlo Séquin, with his restless, investigative mind, has been a constant source of inspiration for me, greatly helping me in all aspects of my doctoral research. He also extensively reviewed this thesis, suggesting many improvements, and teaching me the art of best organizing the exposition of technical material. Dave Patterson, the leader of the RISC project, and the one responsible for its success, was our main driving force, judiciously guiding the choice of the reduced instruction set and the making of many design decisions, organizing the 4-course sequence where the initial study of the RISC concept was carried out, and successfully coordinating the many people and groups that were working on RISC. Bob Sherburne, finally, is the person with whom I spent long days, designing, laying-out, debugging, and testing the RISC II chip; it is with his deep knowledge of IC design, and with his dedicated collaboration that we were able to make the RISC II chip a working, high-performance reality.

There are several other people that I would like to thank a lot. Among them are: John Ousterhout, who created, maintained, and revised *Caesar,* our principal design tool; Lloyd Dickman, who originally suggested the use of a three-stage pipeline; Dan Fitzpatrick and John Foderaro, who helped with design tools and with software problems; And Kjell Doksum, Brian Reid, Veneta, and Marina, who all helped me, in their own way, during some crucial points of the preparation of this work.

Reduced Instruction Set

Computer Architectures for VLSI

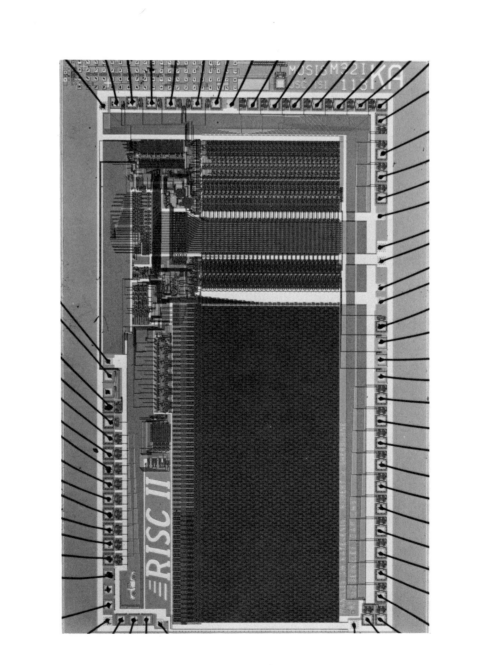

Chapter 1

Introduction

Even in Very Large Scale Integrated (VLSI) circuits, the number of transistors available on a single chip must be considered a limited resource. In the course of the "Reduced Instruction Set Computer" (RISC) project at U. C. Berkeley, it was found that hardware support for complex instructions is not the most effective way of utilizing the transistors in a VLSI processor. In chapter 1, the RISC concept is presented first, followed by an overview of the Berkeley RISC project, and some notes on the organization of this book.

1.1 The RISC Concept:
Effective Use of Scarce Hardware Resources

Increasing the size or complexity of a digital circuit may either enhance or impair the overall system performance, depending on how judiciously the added complexity is chosen. The Berkeley RISC project has demonstrated the viability of general purpose computers with simple instruction sets. It has brought concrete evidence showing the non-optimal utilization of silicon resources in most contemporary single-chip processors, due to the increased complexity of their instruction sets.

1.1.1 Size, Complexity, and Speed

Increasing the size or complexity of a digital circuit may lead to better system performance. For example:

- A 32-bit adder will allow a 32-bit processor to operate at higher speed than a 16-bit adder, used twice for each addition, would allow it to operate.
- Overlapping instruction execution with the fetching of the next instruction reduces the execution time of programs with an average number of jump instructions.
- Including, for example, 4 registers into a general-purpose CPU will give a much better performance than if only 2 registers were included, -- if the compiler can take advantage of additional registers.

All these are examples of cases where the increase in size or complexity is used to allow parallel execution of common parallel operations, or to provide faster access to frequently used operands.

On the other hand, increasing the size or complexity of a digital circuit can also have negative effects on its performance:

- A larger size entails longer wire delays.
- More gates mean less power is available per gate, resulting in reduced driving strength.
- A more complex mode of operation usually means interposing more circuit elements in the path of information flow: for example, additional or larger input multiplexors, increased output fanout, or more circuits hanging off busses. This inevitably reduces the maximum possible operating speed.

In VLSI systems this trade-off between speed and size/complexity of a circuit is more pronounced than it is in the previous-generation systems built from TTL SSI/MSI parts. The following tables show typical capacitances and delay times in the TTL technology and in the NMOS process by which RISC II was fabricated:

Typical Delays of TTL inverters (7404) or 3-state buffers (74240):		
	S-series	LS-series
$C_L=15pF$	3 ns	10 ns
$C_L=50pF$	5 ns	15 ns

Typical Delays of 4μm NMOS inverters or buffers:		
	high-power	low-power
$C_L=0.1pF$	3 ns	10 ns
$C_L=2.5pF$	15 ns	60 ns

In VLSI MOS technologies, the gate delays vary over much wider ranges than in discrete technologies. The reason is twofold. On the one hand, the load capacitance significantly influences the delay time of MOS gates, while for discrete parts a large portion of the delay is due to the internal circuitry and to the package and does not depend so strongly on C_L. On the other hand, custom MOS offers much wider design choices in terms of size of devices, type of circuits available, and size of load to be driven. Thus, the dependence of system speed on size and complexity is much more direct in VLSI than it is in older, discrete technologies.

Another important factor in VLSI system design is the large difference in available bandwidth between on-chip and off-chip communication. In today's (1983) technology, one may typically see transfers on the order of 200 bits every 20 ns on-chip, versus only 50 bits going through the chip periphery every 50 ns. This character of the chip periphery as communications bottleneck makes it desirable to pack as much functionality as possible into the restricted area of a single chip. In this context, an increase of the size and complexity of one circuit feature may only be achieved at the expense of another.

Taking these trade-offs between size/complexity and speed properly into account, leads to hierarchically organized systems, where the inner units are physically smaller and support the most frequent operations. The system's architect has the important role of selecting the functions to be supported at the various levels of the system's hierarchy. This is particularly important in VLSI system design, where the spectrum of possible choices is wider and more continuous than it is in systems employing discrete technology.

1.1.2 Recent Trends, and the RISC Alternative

A general trend in computers today is to increase the complexity of architectures commensurate with the increasing potential of implementation technologies, as exemplified by the complex successors of simpler machines. Compare, for example, the DEC VAX-11 to the PDP-11 [Stre78], the IBM System/38 to the System/3 [Utle78], and the Intel iAPX-432 to the 8086 [Tyne81] [Orga82].

Following the discussion made in the previous subsection, it is necessary to study the overall effect of such complex instruction sets on performance. For a VLSI system, does this approach lead to an effective utilization of the scarce silicon resources? In 1980, the "Reduced Instruction Set Computer" (RISC) project was started at U. C. Berkeley, with the goal of investigating an alternative to this trend. The hypothesis was that, since complex instructions are rarely used by actual programs, their inclusion into the processor's instruction set has more negative effects on overall performance than it has positive ones. On the other hand, the frequent program accesses to operands justify better support than is normally available in traditional architectures. A third consideration was that a simplifyed architecture is important in a field of such a rapidly changing technology, because it leads to a short design and debugging time, thus allowing quick exploitation of the new technologies.

From these considerations the Berkeley RISC Architecture was derived. It specified a general purpose processor with simple instructions and with many registers organized in multiple register banks. The RISC project has now (1983) demonstrated not only the viability but also the very definite advantages of this approach. The judicious choice of the instruction set was a key to this success. First, the most necessary and frequent operations (instructions) in programs were identified. Then, the data-path and timing required for their execution was identified. And last, other *frequent* operations (instructions), which *could also fit* into that data-path and timing, were included into the instruction set.

During the definition of the RISC architecture, its implementation was kept in mind at all times. The resulting architecture lies on a "knee of the curve" of the speed-versus-complexity trade-off. A significant number of commonly-used instructions is included in the ISP description of RISC (§ 3.1); all of them are implementable with a simple data-path and timing scheme. Including more instructions into the ISP would have required significant changes to the hardware, thus slowing down the cycle time.

U. C. Berkeley is not the only place where research on simple instruction sets is going on. Similar investigations are being carried out at IBM Watson Research Center in the 801 project [Radi82], and at Stanford University in the MIPS project [Henn82] [Henn83].

1.2   Evolution of the Berkeley RISC Project

Table 1.2.1 shows the key steps in the history of the Berkeley RISC project. Two faculty members and about two dozen graduate students have been involved in this three-year project. The author of this dissertation has been heavily involved in it, starting with the architectural studies in the spring of 1980; subsequently his main concern was focused on the definitions of the micro-architectures for both NMOS versions and on design, layout, and debugging of RISC II.

The Berkeley RISC architecture was defined in 1980, after extensive architectural studies performed during a graduate course. These included the measurement of several program parameters, such as the number of various statements and addressing modes, usage of local scalars, and procedure nesting depth. The measurements were done mostly in C, and also in Pascal, and did *not* include any numeric computations program. This is the applications area for which the RISC architecture was designed. The author of this dissertation contributed to the above studies with a preliminary look at the data-path and the timing for such an architecture. Once the architectural design was finalized, he defined a micro-architecture to implement it. This was described in detail in [Kate80], and was subsequently adopted by a group of 5 graduate students who designed, laid-out,

Table 1.2.1: History of the RISC Project.		
Period	Activity	People
wint.80	RISC idea	Patterson, Séquin
spr.80	Architectural Studies	Patterson, 15 gr. st.
sumr.80	Architecture Definition	Patterson, 4 gr. stud.
sumr.-fall.80	Compiler, Assem., Simul.	Campbell, Tamir
sumr.-fall.80	RISC I Micro-Architecture	Katevenis
wint.81	RISC II Micro-Architecture	Katevenis
wint.-spr.81	RISC I Design & Layout	Fitzpatrick, Foderaro, Peek,Peshkess, VanDyke
sum.81-sp.82	RISC I fabrication	MOSIS, XEROX
sumr.82	RISC I tested	Foderaro, VanDyke
spr.-sumr.82	RISC I board	VanDyke
wint.81-w.83	RISC II Design & Layout	Katevenis,Sherburne
spr.83	RISC II fabrication	MOSIS, XEROX
sumr.83	RISC II tested	Katevenis,Sherburne
1981-82	RISC/E ECL Paper Design	Beck, Davis, et.al.
spr.-fall.82	I-cache Design & Layout	Hill, Lioupis, Nyberg, Sippel
spr.83	I-cache fabrication	MOSIS, XEROX
sumr.83	I-cache tested	Lioupis, Hill
fall.82-fall.83	CMOS RISC Layout Study	Takada
wint.83-ong.	RISC II microcomputer	Lioupis, Campbell

and debugged the corresponding NMOS IC in only six months. It was originally called "RISC I Gold", and later on simply "RISC I". Its very short design time was due to the simplicity of the architecture [Fitz81]. It was fabricated and tested; the chips were functionally correct, but slower than intended by about a factor of 4 [FoVP82]. This was due to a lack of tools, at that time, that could find all the critical timing paths in a simulation of the whole chip. A RISC I board, with memory and I/O around the CPU chip, was built by VanDyke and used to demonstrate the execution of small programs.

In parallel with the design of RISC I, the present author defined a second, more ambitious micro-architecture for the same processor architecture, and subsequently implemented it, together with Robert Sherburne, by designing, laying-out, and debugging a second NMOS IC. This was originally called "RISC I Blue", and later on "RISC II". It was fabricated and tested in 1983. The chips are functionally correct and work very close to predicted speed. RISC II occupies 25% less silicon area than RISC I, even though it has 75% more registers. This was made possible by reducing the number of busses that go through the register file from three to two, which led to a much more compact register cell. To avoid a resulting performance loss, an additional pipeline stage was used, as suggested by Lloyd Dickman. Overall, the circuit design and layout for RISC II was done with careful attention to performance.

Other parts of the RISC project have been going on in parallel: A detailed paper design was made for RISC/E, a RISC CPU and cache memory made out of SSI/MSI ECL IC's [Blom83]. Another group designed and laid-out an Instruction-Cache chip for the RISC II CPU [Patt83]. Cache chips were fabricated and tested; they were found to be functionally correct and to work very close to the predicted speed. A CMOS version of the RISC II micro-architecture was studied by M. Takada by designing and laying-out the data-path and most of the control. Finally, there is ongoing work, by Lioupis originally [Liou83] and by Campbell now, for designing and building a micro-computer around the RISC II CPU and I-cache chips.

1.3   Book Organization

Since it is crucial for an architect to know which are the most frequently used operations (instructions), chapter 2 reviews the relevant literature on program measurements and complements it by a study of program properties done with a different method, providing yet another point of view.

The next three chapters deal with the architecture, micro-architecture, design, layout, debugging, and testing of RISC II. They show how the Berkeley RISC architecture fits into the concept of effective utilization of the hardware resources, and they present the most important experiences gained and conclusions reached from the whole cycle of micro-architecture definition to design, layout, debugging, and testing. It is appropriate here to make a clarification as to the terminology used. The term "RISC architecture" is general and refers to any architecture inspired by the "RISC concept" as presented in section 1.1. The term "the Berkeley RISC architecture" refers to the specific RISC architecture defined at U.C.Berkeley in 1980 and implemented by RISC I and RISC II; sometimes we may abusively use the shorter term "*the* RISC architecture" to refer to it.

The book concludes with a projection into the future. Soon, VLSI chips will have significantly more transistors than were used by RISC I or RISC II. What will these additional transistor be used for? Chapter 6 proposes additional hardware organizations, always within the framework of simple instruction sets, which will make effective use of those transistors for speeding up the execution of general-purpose computations.

Chapter 2

The Nature
of General-Purpose Computations

In the design of a computer system, two issues must be studied carefully:

(1) FUNCTION: What is the purpose of the computer system? What is the nature of the computations it will perform? What are the necessary features that will enable it to perform those computations with high efficiency?

(2) COST: Can the desirable architectural features be implemented at a reasonable cost and with a reasonable performance, in a particular technology? What are the trade-offs imposed by the constraints of a given implementation technology?

   This chapter focuses on the first question of what it is that computer systems usually do, leaving the bulk of the discussion on implementation issues for the next chapters. We are interested in "general-purpose computer systems". Although it is difficult to define this term, we use it to refer to systems not biased towards the execution of a particular algorithm, and, specifically, systems that execute a mix of word processing, data base applications, mail and communications, compilations, CAD, control, and numerical applications. The chapter will assemble a picture of the nature of such "general-purpose" computations, by collecting program measurements from the literature, and by studying the critical loops of some representative programs. The resulting picture will be used in the next chapters.

2.1   Goal and Methods of Program Measurement

The main vehicle for a qualitative and quantitative understanding of the nature of computations is the measurement of the important properties on some real programs. It is very difficult for such a study to be made *abstractly* -- not in connection with a particular model of computers and computations, because real programs and programming languages *are* written and defined with a particular model in mind, and because the properties to be measured depend on this model.

Throughout this dissertation, a *von Neumann model* of computers and computations is assumed. Programs written in corresponding languages are considered in this chapter. C and FORTRAN program fragments are studied, and measurements from the literature are reported, which were collected by looking at programs written in FORTRAN, XPL, PL/I, Algol, Pascal, C, BLISS, Basic, and SAL. This section identifies the main properties of computations which are important in the design of von Neumann architectures, and lists tools and methods for their measurement.

2.1.1   Architecturally Important Properties of Computations

In the von Neumann model, computations are performed by sequentially executing operations on operands which are kept in a storage device. The sequence of operations is dynamically controlled by operand values. Thus, the properties of computations that will interest us are:

- **Operands used.** Their type, size, structure, and the nature of their usage determines the storage organization for keeping them and the addressing modes for accessing them. In particular:

    - Constant or variable operands.
    - Types of operands: integers, floating-point, characters, pointers.
    - Structure of operands: scalars, arrays, strings, structures of records.
    - Declaration of operands: globals, procedure arguments, procedure locals.
    - Number of operands, sizes, and frequency of accesses for the above categories.

- Amount and nature of locality-of-reference, possibly determined individually for each one of the above categories, for example, for scalars, arrays, (dynamic) structures, globals, and procedure activation records.

- **Operations performed.** These will determine the required operational units, and their connection to the storage units. The relative frequency of operations such as the ones listed below is important, and the variation of those frequencies with the operands' categories is also of interest.

  - Test, compare, add, subtract, multiply, divide, and so on.
  - Operation type, such as integer, floating-point, or string.
  - Higher level operations, such as I/O, buffer, list, and so forth.

- **Execution sequencing.** This will determine the control and pipeline organization:

  - Control transfers: conditional/unconditional jumps, calls, returns. What is their frequency, distance, conditions, predictability, and earliness of condition resolution.
  - Amount and nature of extractable parallelism. This is a very general and important question; for von Neumann architectures, we are interested in low-level parallelism.

While quantitative measurements are essential, the large number of properties to be measured -- especially if correlation among them is also studied -- makes a qualitative understanding of the global picture equally important. Methods for both kinds of analysis are presented below.

2.1.2 Static and Dynamic Measurements

Program measurements are usually collected by running the program under study through a suitable filter, or by executing it in a suitable environment. In both cases the result of this processing is a count of the numbers of times that some feature has appeared or that some particular property has held true in the text of the program or in its execution.

Measurements referring to the text of a program are called static. They give no useful information on performance, because they are not weighted relative to the number of times each statement was executed. They can show the size of storage required for the machine code and for the statically allocated objects, and they can show what the compiler has to deal with. Under crude assumptions, the static characteristics of programs can also give some indication on their dynamic behaviour.

Measurements referring to the execution of a program are called dynamic. Execution of the program requires previous compilation into object code for some machine, except if expensive interpretation is used. Thus, dynamic measurements usually refer to machine rather than source code, introducing another - often unwanted - parameter into the study. Machine code can be correlated back to source code, so that dynamic measurements at the source level can be inferred. However, this correlation is not always easy or precise.

Static and dynamic program measurements have frequently appeared in the literature, and have also been collected early in the RISC project (spring 1980). Section 2.2 reviews some of them.

2.1.3 Source-Code Profiling and Studying

Because the list of important properties of computations is very long, and because several of them are difficult to quantify or to measure, the static and dynamic program measurements have some limitations. There is another method of looking at the nature of computations which is less quantitative but more qualitative, and which can complement these measurements or give a better idea of what specific other measurements should be taken. That method is to carefully study the source code of a program and, if possible, the underlying algorithms, concentrating on those portions of it which account for most of the execution time.

It has been observed, time and again, that programs spend most of their execution time in small portions of their code, the so-called "critical loops". This makes it feasible and worthwhile to study those portions in detail, to understand the nature and properties of the computation that is carried out. The critical loops can be identified by profiling the program during execution. Profiling is the dynamic measurement of how much of the execution "cost" is spent at each place in the program's code. The "cost" may be:

- time spent,
- number of source-code lines executed,
- number of memory accesses, and so forth.

In section 2.3 we will study some critical loops that have been identified by other researchers. Section 2.4 studies some more critical loops, which were identified by this author using two profiling systems. The first was the standard profiling facility of UNIX: compilation using the *-p* or *-pg* switch, execution, and then interpretation of the results by the *prof* or *gprof* program. This method arranges that the program-counter of an executing process be sampled at "random" intervals (on clock interrupts, every 1/60th of a second). The sampled value is used to determine which procedure was executing at that time. If a program runs for a long time, the above samples can be used to construct estimates of how much time was spent in each of the program's procedures. There is no straightforward way to find out the time spent in executing any smaller program portions.

The second profiling system that was used, for programs written in C, belongs to Bell Laboratories (Murray Hill), and was used under special authorization [Wein]. It counts the number of times that each source-code line is executed (but gives no indication as to how long its execution takes). A special version of the C compiler is used, which inserts code at appropriate locations to increment appropriate counters. At the end of execution the counts are saved in a file. Another program is then invoked to correlate those counts with the original source code, and to generate an annotated program listing †.

---

† the count is not always what one would expect for lines like: " } else { ". The listings in section 2.4 have been corrected by hand in those situations.

2.2   Review of some Program Measurements
from the Literature

In this section interesting program measurements from the literature are
reviewed. Measurements on all properties mentioned in section 2.1.1 are not
present here, because some of them either have not received enough attention in
the literature, or were difficult to measure. The measurements were selected
from:

[AlWo75]: Alexander and Wortman collected static and dynamic measurements
from 19 programs (mostly compilers), written in XPL and executed
on the IBM/360 architecture.

[Elsh76]: Elshoff presented static measurements of 120 commercial, production PL/I programs for business data processing.

[HaKe80],

[TaSe83]: Halbert and Kessler, in their study of multiple overlapping windows
early during the RISC project, collected dynamic measurements on
the number of arguments and local scalars per procedure, and on the
locality property of procedure-nesting-depth. They measured the C
compiler, the Pascal interpreter, the troff typesetter, and 6 other
smaller non-numeric programs (all written in C). Tamir and Séquin
collected some more dynamic data on the locality of nesting depth,
measuring the RISC C compiler, the towers-of-Hanoi program, and
the Puzzle program (all written in C).

[Lund77]: Lunde used the concept of "register-lives" in his measurements. He
analyzed half a dozen numeric-computation programs written in 5
different HLL's (2 FORTRAN versions, Basic, Algol, BLISS), plus
some compilers, all running on a DECsystem10 architecture.

[Shus78]: Shustek studied the usage made of the PDP-11 addressing modes, by
statically measuring 10,000 lines of code of an operating system.

[PaSe82]: Patterson and Séquin presented the most important measurements
collected during the early stages of the RISC project, in spring 1980,
in collaboration with E. Cohen and N. Soiffer. Measurements are
dynamic, and were collected from compilers, typesetters, and programs for CAD, sorting, and file comparison. Four of those were

written in C, and the other four in Pascal.

[Tane78]: Tanenbaum published static and dynamic measurements of HLL constructs, collected from more than 300 procedures used in operating-system programs and written in a language that supports structured programming (SAL).

2.2.1 Measurements on Operations

The operations performed by programs are the most frequent object of measurement, in the form of statement types (source level) or opcodes (machine level). The following tables summarize such measurements.

Property:	Measurement:	Reference:
Dynamically executed instructions:		
moves between registers and memory	40 %	[Lund77,p.149]
branching instructions	30 %	(numeric &
fixed-point add/sub's	12 %	compilers)
load, load address	33 %	[AlWo75]
(more than normal, due to 360 archit.)		(mostly compil.
store	10 %	in XPL
branch	14 %	on IBM/360)
compare	6 %	
Statically counted HLL statements:		
assignments	42 %	[AlWo75]
if	13 %	(mostly compil.
call	13 %	in XPL)

Dynamically executed HLL statements:

assignments	42 ± 12 %	[PaSe82]
if	36 ± 15 %	(non-numeric,
call/return	14 ± 4 %	in C & Pascal)
loops	4 ± 3 %	

....weighted with the number of machine instructions executed for each:

loops	37 ± 5 %	[PaSe82]
call/return	32 ± 12 %	(non-numeric,
if	16 ± 7 %	in C & Pascal)
assign	13 ± 4 %	

....weighted with the number of memory accesses necessary for each:

call/return	45 ± 16 %	[PaSe82]
loops	30 ± 4 %	(non-numeric,
assign	15 ± 5 %	in C & Pascal)
if	10 ± 4 %	

More on procedure calls:

procedure calls as percentage of dynamically executed HLL statm.	12 %	[Tane78] (O.S., structured pr.)
procedure call administration as percentage of execution time	25 %	[Lund77,p.151] (BLISS compiler)
an amazing exception case:		[Elsh76] (PL/I
procedures def. within 100 K statm.	83 (only!)	business prog.,
perc. of calls relative to all statem.	2 % (!)	static)

Other frequent high-level operations:

• vector operations (inner product, move, sum, search,...)	[Lund77]
• character-string ops (table-controlled substitute, delete, branch)	
• loop control (incr. a reg., compare it to another reg., and branch)	

Jump distance, measured dynamically:

< 128 bytes	55 %	[AlWo75]
< 16 Kbytes	93 %	

Jump conditions, measured dynamically:

unconditional jumps as % of all jumps	55 %	[AlWo75]
..."the comparison of two non-zero values is about twice as common as compr. with zero".		[Lund77]

Expressions, register lives:

one-term expressions in assignments†	66 %	[Tane78]
two-term expressions in assignments†	20 %	(dynamic)
operators per expression (average)	0.76	[AlWo75](st)
relative to all register lives:		
lives w. no arith. performed on them	50% (20-90%)	[Lund77]
lives w. max†† integer add/sub on them	25% (1-70%)	(dynamic,
lives w. max†† integer mult/div on them	5% (2-20%)	numeric &
lives used in floating-point operations	15% (0-40%)	compilers)
lives used for indexing	40% (20-70%)	[Lund77]

† on the right-hand-side of assignments.

†† "maximum-complexity" operation performed on the register,
   where int-add/sub < int-mult/div < floating-point-op.

These measurements are not very helpful in understanding the high-level nature of computations, but they do show:

- The importance of the procedure call mechanism, since so much time is spent in it.

- The importance of the sequencing control mechanism (compare and branch), since loops and if's are so frequent.

- The importance of simple arithmetic and of addressing, accessing, and moving operands around, since expressions are usually very short, and since half of the operands appearing in registers ("register lives" in [Lund77]) have no arithmetic performed on them.

2.2.2 Measurements on Operands

Measurements on the operands in programs have not been so frequent in the
literature, even though this subject is very important. Lunde [Lund77] measured
on a DECsystem10 that each instruction on the average references 0.5 operands
in memory and 1.4 in registers dynamically. These figures depend highly on the
architecture and on the compiler, but they do illustrate, nevertheless, the importance of fast operand accessing, since that occurs so frequently.

Property:	Measurement:	Reference:
Dynamic percentage of operands (HLL):		
integer constants	20 ± 7 %	[PaSe82]
scalars	55 ± 11 %	(non-numeric,
array/structure	25 ± 14 %	in C & Pascal)
local-scalar references as percentage of all scalar references	> 80 %	[PaSe82]
global-array/structure references as percentage of all arr/str. references	> 90 %	[PaSe82]
Use of PDP-11 addressing modes:		
"The 4 most common modes are perhaps the 4 simplest":		[Shus78]
register	32 %	(static,
indexed (e.g. for fields of structures)	17 %	O.S.)
immediate (constants)	15 %	
PC-relative (direct addressing)	11 %	
all others	25 %	
"The 4 least-used modes are precisely the 4 memory indirect ones (1%)".		
"Half of the move instr. had a register as their dest."		[Shus78]
"Half of the compare/add/subtract instructions had one of their operands be an immediate"		

A property that had attracted very little attention in the past is the high locality of references to local scalar variables. The figures from [PaSe82] given above

show that over half of the accesses to non-constant values are made to local scalars. On top of that, references to arrays/structures require a previous reference to their index or pointer, which is again a - usually local - scalar. Most of the time, the number of local scalars per procedure is small.

Tanenbaum [Tane78] found that 98 % of the dynamically called procedures had less than 6 arguments, and that 92 % of them had less than 6 local scalar variables. Similar numbers were found by Halbert and Kessler:

Procedure Activation Records: [HaKe80] Percentage of executed procedure calls with:		
	compiler, interpr. and typesetter	other smaller programs (non-numer.)
> 3 arguments	0 to 7 %	0 to 5 %
> 5 arguments	0 to 3 %	0 %
> 8 words of arg's & locals	1 to 20 %	0 to 6 %
> 12 words of arg's & locals	1 to 6 %	0 to 3 %

Thus, the number of words per procedure activation is not large. The following measurements show that the number of procedure activations touched during a reasonable time span is not large either. This establishes the locality-of-reference property for local scalars.

Locality of Procedure Nesting Depth: [HaKe80] [TaSe83] Percentage of executed procedure calls which overflow from last span of nesting depths:		
(assuming that the span of nesting depths has constant size, and that its position moves by one on every over/under-flow; this corresponds to a RISC register file with as many windows as the span size, and with no window reserved for interrupts. See section 3.2).		
	2 compilers, interpr. typesetter, Hanoi	6+1 other smaller programs (non-numeric)
span sz = 4 (4 wind.)	8 to 15 %	0 to 2.5 %
span sz = 8 (8 wind.)	1 to 3 %	0 to 0.2 %

2.3   Study of some Critical FORTRAN Loops (collected mostly by Knuth)

Knuth, in [Knut71], presents a study of where FORTRAN programs spend most of their time. The programs he measured varied from text-editing to scientific number-crunching programs. Dynamic measurements of the HLL statements executed showed that:

- 67% were assignments,
- one third of those assignments were of the type A=B,
- 11% were IF, 9% were GOTO, 3% were DO,
- 3% were CALL, and 3% were RETURN,
- More than 25% of the execution time was spent in I/O formatting.

However, what is most interesting for our study is that he gives the actual code fragments where 17 of those programs (chosen at random) spent most of their time. He used those fragments ("examples") to test the effectiveness of various techniques for optimization of compiled code. We will briefly study those same examples from our point of interest: understanding the nature of computations, and in particular answering the questions of section 2.1.1. The 17 examples have been classified in three categories of array-numeric, array-searching, and miscellaneous style examples. Their code (or a summary of it) is given below in a modernized-FORTRAN format. An eighteenth example of a critical loop, collected by the author of this dissertation, was added to the first category. It is the main loop of a procedure that inverts a positive-definite symmetric matrix. It was included in the study after two researchers in structural mechanics and in fluid dynamics independently told this author that they felt matrix inversion was the most time-consuming computation done by people in their area.

2.3.1 "Array-Numeric" Style Examples

Example 3:
```
double A, B, D
do 1 k=1,N
1   A = T[I-k, 1+k] ; B = T[I-k, J+k] ; D = D - A*B
```

Example 7:
```
do 1 i=1,N
    A = X**2 + Y**2 - 2.*X*Y*C[i]
1   B = SQRT(A) ; K = 100.*B+1.5 ; D[i] = S[i]*T[K]
    Q = D[1] - D[N]
    do 2 i=2,M,2
2   Q = Q + 4.*D[i] + 2.*D[i+1]
```

Example 9:
```
do 2 k=1,M
do 2 j=1,M
initialize...
do 1 i=1,M
    N = j + j + (i-1)*M2 ; B = A[k,i]
1   X = X + B*Z[N] ; Y = Y + B*Z[N-1]
2 more computations...
```

Example 11:   a Fast Fourier Transform. It computes sums and products of floating-point elements of two linear arrays. One array is

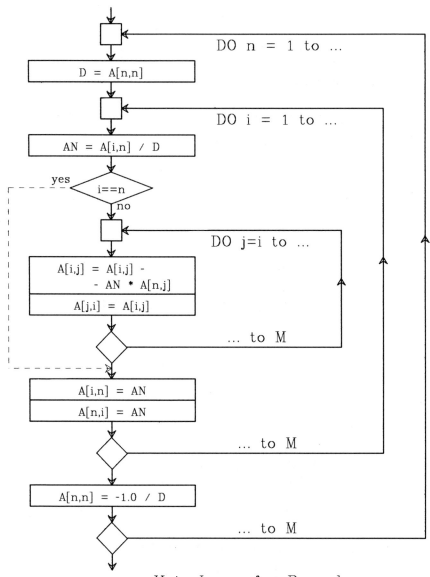

Figure 2.3.1:   Main Loop of a Procedure
                     to Invert a Positive-Definite
                     Symmetric Matrix.

accessed sequentially, and the other one with a step of N.

Example 12:   a very long inner loop, with counter arithmetic, array accesses (many 3-dimensional arrays, some 2- and 1- dimensional), and floating-point multiplications and additions. There is one expression with 32 operators! In spite of its heavy computation character, this program has no more floating-point operations than it has simple counter and index operations.

Example 15:   do 1 j=i,N
                      H[i,j] = H[i,j] + S[i]*S[j]/D1 - S[k+i]*S[k+j]/D2
          1   H[j,i] = H[i,j]

Example 17:   do 1 i=1,N
          1   A = A + B[i] + C[k+i]

Example - Matrix Inversion:
        Figure 2.3.1 shows the aforementioned critical loop of positive-definite symmetric matrix inversion, in an abstract flow-chart form.

All these critical loops are of the same style: They perform floating-point operations on elements of arrays. Two almost independent "processes" exist. First, array elements are accessed in a *regular* fashion, i.e. in an arithmetic progression of memory addresses; the loop control is related to the array indexes, and does not depend on the array data. The second "process" is that of doing the actual numerical data computations.

2.3.2 "Array-Searching" Style Examples

Example 1:   a search for the maximum of the absolute values:
             do 2 j=1,N
               t = ABS(A[i,j]) ; if (t>s) then s=t ;
          2   continue

Example 2:   a search for a match:
```
     do 1 j=38,53
        if (K[i]==L[j]) then goto 2
 1   continue
```

Example 10:
```
     do 1 i=L,M
 1   if ( X[i-1,j] < Q  and  X[i,j] ≥ Q ) then rare
```

Example 13:   a binary search:
```
 1   j = (i+k)/2
     if (j==i) then  goto 2
     if ( X[j] == XKEY )  then  goto 3
     if ( X[j] < XKEY )  then  i=j else  k=j
     goto 1
```

These examples are non-numeric. Most of them access the array(s) in a regular manner, like the examples in 2.3.1. However, the control of their sequencing is *dynamic* in nature: it depends on the actual data being visited, rather than on regularly incremented counters.

2.3.3 "Miscellaneous" Style Examples

Example 4:   first a poor quality random-number generator is defined:
```
     subroutine RAND(R)
     j = i * 65539
     if (j<0) then  j = j + 2147483647 + 1
     R = j ;  R = R * 0.4656613e-9
     i = j ;  k = k+1 ;  return
```
then it is called:
```
     do 1 k=M,20
        call RAND(R)
 1   if ( R > 0.81 ) then  N[k] = 1
```
Knuth comments: "...the most interesting thing here, however, is the effect of subroutine linkage, since the long prologue and epilogue significantly increase the time of the inner loop".

Example 5:   this is a long inner loop that does lots of floating-point computa-
               tions. It contains some simple arithmetic and compare &
               branch operations on integer counters, sequential addressing of
               two linear arrays, and several floating-point exponentiations,
               multiplications, and additions. The loop is badly written, with
               many large common subexpressions. There is lots of low-level
               parallelism present, mainly among the floating-point computa-
               tions, but also between them and the integer ones.

Example 6:   a subroutine S is defined:
                   subroutine S(A,B,X)
                   dimension A[2], B[2]
                   X=0 ; Y = (B[2]-A[2])*12 + B[1] - A[1]
                   if (Y<0) then goto 1
                   X=Y
                 1   return
               then W is defined, which is called multiple times, and which
               calls S:
                   subroutine W(A,B,C,D,X)
                   dimension A[2], B[2], C[2], D[2], U[2], V[2]
                   X=0 ; call S(A,D,X) ; if (X==0) then goto 3
                   call S(C,B,X) ; if (X==0) then goto 3
                   rarely executed code
                 3   return

Example 8:   subroutine COMPUTE ; common ....
                   complex Y[10], Z[10]
                   R=real(Y[n]) ; P=sin(R) ; Q=cos(R)
                   S = C * 6.0 * (P/3.0 - Q*Q*P)
                   T = 1.414214 * P * P * Q * C * 6.0
                   U=T/2.
                   V = -2.0 * C * 6.0 * (P/3.0 - Q*Q*P/2.0)
                   Z[1] = (0.0,-1.0) * (S*Y[1] + T*Y[2])
                   Z[2] = (0.0,-1.0) * (U*Y[1] + V*Y[2])
                   return

Example 14:   do 1 i=1,N
                1   C = C/D*R ; D = D-1 ; R = R+1

Example 16:   real function F(X)
                    Y = X * 0.7071068
                    if (Y < 0.0) then goto 1
                    rarely executed code
                1   F = 1.0 - 0.5 * (1.0 + ERF(-Y)) ; return

These examples help us remember that real programs are not always as simple and straightforward as those seen in sections 2.3.1 and 2.3.2. Relative to
those simpler ones, these "miscellaneous" programs are characterized by more
numeric computations, the same number or fewer array accesses, less
index/counter arithmetic, less or unusual-style comparisons and branches, and --
in some cases -- more procedure calls.

2.3.4 The Nature of Numeric Computations

The above examples give a picture of typical numeric computations, which can
be summarized as follows:

1. The absolutely predominant data structure is the **array.** Most of the arrays
   are 1- or 2- dimensional. (Of course, the predominance of arrays over other
   data-structures can not be deduced by studying FORTRAN programs, since
   arrays are the only data-structure allowed in that language. However, it is
   known that the vast majority of numerical computations is performed to solve
   engineering or other similar problems, where the array arises as the natural
   data-structure.)

2. In the vast majority of the cases, the array elements are **accessed in regular
   sequence(s).** There are a few "working locations" in the array(s), and their
   addresses change as arithmetic progressions. The step is quite often equal to
   one element size, or, at other times, it is the column size or some other constant.

3. A few integer scalar variables are used as **loop-counters and array-indexes.**
   The arithmetic performed on them is simple and corresponds to the above
   "regular sequence" of array accesses: increment by a constant, compare &

branch. **Address computations** for multi-dimensional arrays require integer multiplication. Most of the times, it is feasible and advantageous for the optimizing compiler (or the very sophisticated programmer) to replace those integer counters/indexes by actual memory pointers; the address computations are avoided in this way (see [AhU177], p.466: Induction Variable Elimination).

4. The numeric computations are usually **floating-point operations** (multiplications and additions/subtractions being the most frequent). Several such operations are performed, but usually not many more in number than the integer operations on counters.

5. **Low-level parallelism** is present in many cases, and has two forms: (1) among various floating-point operations, usually when long expressions are computed, and when a series of assignment statements is executed with no control-transfers in between; and (2) between counter/address calculations and floating-point operations, especially when program sequencing (if's, loop's) depend on the former only. This quite common "static nature" of program sequencing is an important characteristic of programs which perform a certain computation on all elements of a vector or of an array.

6. The last property also gives to these programs significant amounts of **higher-level parallelism.** Subsequent loop iterations are independent and could proceed in parallel. Some times, they are completely independent (Example 15 of section 2.3.1), so that a highly pipelined von Neumann processor could take advantage of them. Other times, they are less independent (Example 17 in section 2.3.1 would require a tree-organized addition); von Neumann architectures and languages typically cannot exploit that parallelism.

2.4   A Study of four C Programs
for Text Processing and CAD of IC's

In this section we study the critical loops of four non-numeric programs, written in C and taken out of the Berkeley UNIX† and CAD environment:

fgrep   the UNIX program which searches a file for occurrences of fixed strings,

sed   the UNIX stream (batch) text editor,

sort   the UNIX program to sort the lines in a file, and

mextra   a circuit extractor [FitzMe] which, given a description of the IC's geometry, generates a list of the transistors and their interconnections present in an integrated circuit. It works by first reading-in the description of the geometry and building a corresponding dynamic data structure, and then "scanning" the IC following horizontal scan-lines of gradually increasing y-coordinate. It may be considered an example of a program that *manipulates a nontrivial dynamic data structure.*

As an argument in support of the representativeness of the above sample of programs, let us look at a typical compiler. Kessler's Pascal compiler spends most of its time [Kess82] scanning the input (i.e. reading and recognizing characters), generating assembly code (i.e. character I/O), and walking through tree structures and interrogating them. These functions are similar to what *fgrep, sed,* and *mextra* do.

The tools described in section 2.1.3 were used for locating the critical loops. Below, wherever code is shown, the number on the left of each line is the count of how many times the line was executed during the test run.

---

†UNIX is a trademark of Bell Laboratories.

2.4.1 FGREP: a String Search Program

In the test run, *fgrep* was used to search for occurrences of the string "kateveni" in a file of size ≈ 230 KBytes (there were a few hundred such occurrences). The run took about 6 seconds CPU time, allocated as follows:

- ≈ 87% in the procedure *execute()*,
- ≈ 11% in _read (i.e. in the operating system),
- ≈ 2% in everything else.

The procedure *execute()* follows:

---

fgrep: execute() [87%]:

```
  | # define ccomp(a,b) (yflag ? lca(a)==lca(b) : a==b)
  | # define lca(x) (isupper(x) ? tolower(x) : x)
  |
  | struct words {
  |      char inp, out;
  |      struct words *nst, *link, *fail;
  | } w[MAXSIZ];
  | int    yflag;
  |
  | ....
  |
1 | execute(file)   char *file;
  | { register struct words  *c;
  |   register int  ccount;
  |   register char  ch, *p;
  |   char  buf[2*BUFSIZ];
  |   int  f, failed;  char *nlp;
  |
```

1	|	.... *Initial Set-Up Work* ....
229253	|	for (;;)
229253	|	{ if (--ccount <= 0)
226	|	{ *read-in a new 1Kbyte block or exit loop* }

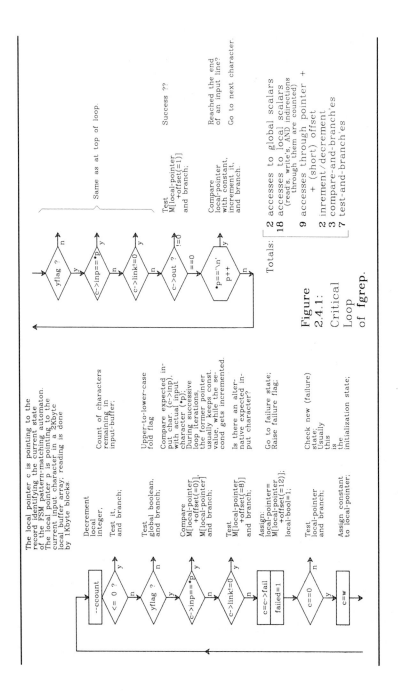

Figure
2.4.1:
Critical
Loop
of **fgrep**.

```
          |          nstate:
229252 |          if (ccomp(c->inp, *p))    /* in-line expansion */
   923 |              {  c = c->nst; }
228329 |          else if (c->link != 0)
     0 |              {  c = c->link; goto nstate; }
          |          else
228329 |              {  c = c->fail;
228329 |                  failed = 1;
228329 |                  if (c==0)
228329 |                      {  c = w;
          |                      istate:
228329 |                      if (ccomp(c->inp,*p))  /*in-line exp*/
     0 |                          {  c = c->nst; }
228329 |                      else if (c->link != 0)
     0 |                          {  c=c->link; goto istate; }
          |                      }
     0 |                      else goto nstate;
          |                  }
229252 |          if (c->out)
    48 |              {  Code for Success  }
229204 |          if (*p++ == '\n')
  4237 |              {  Code for End-of-Line  }
          |          }
     1 |      ....  Final Wrap-Up Work ....
      | }
```

Figure 2.4.1 contains a flow-chart of the critical loop of this run of *fgrep*. The vast majority of the operations performed are simply:
• accesses to scalars (mostly locals) and indirections through them to access fields of structures to which they are pointing, and
• comparisons (mostly to zero) & subsequent branches. The high frequency of compare-&-branches is in part a result of the nature of the program (pattern matching), but is also a general characteristic of the non-numeric programs, as the next examples will show.

2.4.2 SED: a Batch Text Editor

In our test run, *sed* copies a 2.2 Mbyte file to output, searching for occurrences
of three short fixed patterns. It replaces two of them with 2 others (one shorter,
one longer), and upon encountering the third one, it appends a specified new line
after the current one. The run took about 160 sec CPU time, allocated as follows:

- ≈ 23% in the procedure *execute()*,
- ≈ 23% in the procedure *match()*,
- ≈ 16% in the procedure *gline()*, and
- all other procedures accounted for < 8% each.

---

sed: execute() [23%]:

```
      1 | execute(file)      char *file;
        | { register char  *p1, *p2;
        |   register union reptr *ipc;
        |   int  c;   char *execp;
        |
      1 | .... Initial Set-Up Work...
  52820 |   for(;;)
  52820 |    { if((execp = gline(linebuf)) == badp) { rare }
  52819 |      spend = execp;
 158457 |      for(ipc = ptrspace; ipc->command; )
 158457 |         { p1 = ipc->ad1;
 158457 |           p2 = ipc->ad2;
 158457 |           if(p1)
  52819 |              { if(ipc->inar) { never }
  52819 |                else if(*p1 == CEND) { never }
  52819 |                else if(*p1 == CLNUM) { never }
  52819 |                else if(match(p1, 0)) {22,000 if's exct'd}
  30899 |                else {62,000 stmnts exect'd; continue;}
        |              }
 127558 |           if(ipc->negfl) { never }
 127558 |           command(ipc);
```

```
127558 |                if(delflag) { never }
127558 |                if(jflag) { never }
127558 |                else  ipc++;
       |            }
 52819 |        if(!nflag && !delflag)
2143025 |            {  for(p1 = linebuf; p1 < spend; p1++)
       |                          /*"spend" is a global pointer*/
2143025 |                putc(*p1, stdout);
```
/*Note: in-line expanded to: */
/*   (-- _iob[1]._cnt>=0 ? *(_iob[1]._ptr)++ = *p1 : {rare}) */
/* _iob[1]._cnt, _iob[1]._ptr are global scalars (compiler knows their addr.)*/
```
 52819 |                putc('\n', stdout);
       |            }
 52819 |        if(aptr > abuf) { 22,000 calls: arout(); }
 52819 |        delflag = 0;
       |    }
       | }
```

Here, we have:

- 0.26 M procedure calls,
- 2.35 M compare-&-branch,
- 3.10 M test-&-branch,
- 4.40 M incrementations, and
- 0.50 M assignments with no operation (move-type).

The vast majority of operands are accessed indirectly, through local pointers with a zero or small offset. Other accesses are to local and global scalars. Certainly, a lot of this procedure's time is spent in the tight **for** loop that copies characters to standard output.

sed: match() [23%]:

```
161106 | match(expbuf, gf)    char *expbuf;
```

```
        | { register char      *p1, *p2, c;
        |
161106  |       if(gf) { Execute ≈ 150,000 statements }
158457  |       else { p1 = linebuf; locs = 0; }
161106  |       p2 = expbuf;
161106  |       if(*p2++) { never }
        |       /* fast check for first character: */
161106  |       if(*p2 == CCHR)
161106  |           { c = p2[1];
5242476 |             do { if(*p1 != c) continue;
269623  |                   if(advance(p1, p2)) { infrequent }
5189445 |                } while(*p1++);
108075  |             return(0);
        |           }
     0  |       ...Various others, never executed...
        | }
```

---

sed: gline() [16%]:

```
 52820  | char *gline(addr)   char *addr;
        | { register char *p1, *p2;   register c;
        |       ...Initial  Set-Up Work (100,000 statements total)...
2174691 |       for (;;)
2174691 |           { if (p2 >= ebp) { rare }
2174690 |             if ((c = *p2++) == '\n') { infrequent }
2121871 |             if(c) if(p1 < lbend)
2121871 |                   *p1++ = c;
        |           }
        |       ...Final  Wrap-Up Work (200,000 statements total)...
        | }
```

These two procedures spend most of their time scanning characters.
Match() scans characters searching for some particular one. *Gline()* scans characters copying and checking them.

2.4.3 SORT: an Extreme, but Real Case

The particular sorting program that was studied, namely the one installed on our UNIX machines, spent one third of the test run time in its calls to a trivial procedure *blank( )* used to scan over blanks. Obviously, it is preferable that *blank( )* were defined as a macro, so that it be expanded in-line. The test run consisted of sorting a 2.2 Mbyte file, relative to the second-in-line field and with elimination of duplicates. It took half-an-hour of CPU time.

---

sort: blank() [31%]:

```
26087970 | blank(c)
26087970 | { if(c==' ' || c=='\t')
 6279488 |                  return(1);
19808482 |         else  return(0);
         | }
```

In general, text-processing programs spend a lot of their time in inner loops where they sequentially "walk" through the characters in buffers, copying, comparing, or testing various things.

It is important to notice that programs dealing with text waste a lot of memory bandwidth in the usual architectures, where a full memory word is accessed each time a byte transaction takes place.

Exploitation of parallelism is difficult in these programs, because of the high frequency of conditional branches. The amount of work done between two consecutive branches is usually quite small, with limited parallelism. Parallelism is often available between operations in two different blocks B1 and B2 separated by a conditional branch, where the branch *usually* follows the path that makes B2 execute after B1. Programs are usually written in such a way that execution of B2 cannot start before it is certain that it should start. The programmer could rearrange the code and introduce temporary variables to hold tentative results, but doing so would lead to complicated and hard to maintain programs.

2.4.4 MEXTRA: a Circuit Extraction Program

Mextra's test run consisted of extracting the circuitry in the control section of the
RISC II chip. It took 330 sec CPU time, allocated as follows:

- ≈ 14% in the procedure *ScanSubSwath()*,
- ≈ 11% in the procedure *Propagate()*,
- ≈ 10% in the procedure *alloc()*,
- ≈ 8% in the procedure *EndTrap()*,
- ≈ 5% in the procedure *Free()*, and
- the remaining procedures took < 4% of the total time each.

---

mextra: ScanSubSwath() [14%]:

```
   771 | ScanSubSwath(bin)    int bin;
       | {   int i, newCount, n;
       |    register edge *new,*old,*last, *oldList,*newList;
       |
       |        ...Initial  Set-Up Work (30,000  statements)...
353237 |        while(new != NIL && old != NIL)    /* NIL is 0 */
352466 |           {  if(new->bb.l < old->bb.l) { infrequent }
       |            else
302554 |              {   if(n < old->bb.t)
254342 |                    {  if(last == NIL) { rare }
253628 |                        else {last->next=old; last=old;}
254342 |                        old = oldList;
254342 |                        if (old!=NIL) oldList=old->next;
       |                    }
 48212 |                 else { infrequent }
       |              }
304254 |           if(depth[last->layer] == 0)
140442 |                StartTrap(last->layer,last);
304254 |           if((depth[last->layer] += last->dir) == 0)
139794 |                EndTrap(last->layer,last);
304254 |           nextEnd =
       |             (nextEnd<last->bb.t ? nextEnd : last->bb.t);
```

```
|          }
|          ...Final Wrap-Up Work (250,000 statements)...
|    }
```

This procedure performs extensive list operations, using local pointers. The total operations performed in its critical loop are:

- 0.6 M procedure calls;
- 0.3 M additions (not counting address computations).
- 1.8 M test-&-branches;
- 1.0 M compare-&-branches;
- ≈ 0.6 M accesses to a global scalar (nextEnd);
- 6.5 M accesses to locals (96% of them to pointers)
      (these include accesses for indirecting through them);
- 3.1 M accesses to fields of structures via a local pointer, and
- 1.0 M (random) accesses to a small array *depth[10]*.

The basic pattern of memory accesses is the list traversal, which places a corresponding limit on locality-of-reference. However, during each loop iteration there are 11 accesses to fields of the structures pointed to by "old–>" and by "last–>". Accesses to various fields of the same structure are obviously accesses to neighboring memory locations, since the structure nodes here have a size of 8 words. Moreover, there are repeated accesses to the same field of the same structure, for example ≈ 4 accesses per iteration to "last–>layer".

The available parallelism, is again limited by the high frequency of conditional branches. Some parallelism can be seen between accessing a memory location and computing the effective address for a subsequent memory access. For example:

```
if ( new->bb.l < old->bb.l )
if ( (depth[last->layer] += last->dir) == 0)
```

mextra: Propagate() [11%]:

```
   773 | Propagate(y,yNext)    int y, yNext;
       | { int   layer, height, tempx,tempy;
       |   register segment *above, *below, *next, *poly, *diff;
       |
       |       ...Initial  Set-Up Work (8,000 statements)...
       |       for( above=Above[layer]; above!=NIL;
       |                       above=above->next )
141443 |           {
       |               for(    ; below!=NIL &&
       |                           below->right < above->left;
       |                       below=below->next)
138000 |                   if(below->area != 0) { rare }
       |               for( next=below;
       |                   next!=NIL && next->left <= above->right;
       |                   next=below->next)
136083 |                   { below = next;
136083 |                       if(above->node == 0)
       |                           {
135024 | above->node = below->node;
135024 | above->area = below->area +
       |               height*(above->right – above->left – 1)/100;
135024 | above->perim = below->perim +
       |               2 * (height + above->right – above->left –
       |                   MIN(above->right,below->rig ht) +
       |                   MAX(above->left,below->left) ) / 10;
       |       /* Note: In-line expansions:   */
       |       /*    MIN(x,y) into: (x<y ? x : y) */
       |       /*    MAX(x,y) into: (x<y ? y : x) */
135024 | below->perim = below->area = 0;
       |                           }
       |                       else { rare }
136083 |                   if(below->area != 0) { never }
       |                   }
141443 |               if(above->node == 0) { rare }
       |           }
```

```
    |        ...Final Wrap-Up Work (500,000 statements)...
    | }
```

Here again, extensive list operations are performed. The list-nodes have a size of 8 words, and are accessed via local pointers. During each loop iteration, 16 accesses are made to fields of a certain list-node, and 15 to fields of another. Each individual field is accessed an average of 3 times. This procedure has more numeric computations than the other procedures in this section, but these are still not the dominant factor.

mextra: alloc() [10%]:

```
283165 | alloc(n)
       | { register int tmp; register struct cell *ptr;
       |
283165 |     if(n<CELLSIZE-4) { rare }
283165 |     n = (n+WORDSIZE-1)/WORDSIZE;
       |             /* WORDSIZE is 2 in this example */
283165 |     if(TBLSIZE<=n) { rare }
283138 |     else if(FreeTbl[n]!=0)
258662 |         { ptr = FreeTbl[n];
258662 |           FreeTbl[n] = ptr->next;
258662 |           --FreeCnt[n];
258662 |           if(ptr->status!=FREE || ptr->count!=n) {never}
258662 |           if(FreeCnt[n]!=0)
241417 |               { if(FreeTbl[n]->status!=FREE) {never}
241417 |                 if(FreeTbl[n]->count!=n) {never}
       |               }
       |           else { rare }
       |         }
       |     else { infrequent }
283165 |     ptr->status = ALLOC;
283165 |     ptr->count = n;
283165 |     tmp = (int) ptr;
```

```
283165  |        if (n<TBLSIZE) AllocCnt[n]++;
283165  |        return(tmp+4);
        | }
```

This last procedure has no loop; it is entered many times, and does a little work each time. Besides accessing fields of structures via pointers, it also makes many references to the n-th elements of several arrays. These latter are *not* sequential array-element accesses. However, if the information were kept in a single array of structures, instead of in multiple simple arrays, then the above accesses would all be to neighboring memory locations. Slightly more parallelism can be found here, for example:

{ptr–>status=ALLOC; ptr–>count=n; tmp=(int)ptr; if(n<TBLSIZE)}

Also, notice that the *if's* that lead to *then-clauses* which never get executed are consistency checks, and they could all be done in parallel if the language allowed some way of expressing that.

The overall picture from this CAD program is one of many conditional branches and of many accesses to fields of structures using local pointers pointing to them. Although the application has some arithmetic that needs to be done, it does not play a dominant role. There are very few increment operations, contrary to the previous programs studied in earlier sections, because this program deals with dynamic data structures. The locality-of-references to the elements of the data structures stems from the computation pattern of performing several accesses to various fields of a few structure instances, before interest shifts to some new such instances.

2.5   Summary of Findings

In this chapter, we first reviewed static and dynamic program statistics collected by other researchers. Their results indicate that the simplest operations are also the ones that are executed most of the time.

Then, we looked at several FORTRAN programs, most of them doing numerical computations. We observed that they perform primarily floating-point arithmetic operations on operands which frequently are elements of arrays. The inner loops usually traverse the arrays in a "regular" fashion, using indexes that are incremented by a constant amount and compared to a limit. The use of pointers rather than indexes, by the programmer or by the optimizing compiler, would be advantageous.

Then, we studied some text-processing programs written in C, and saw that they spend a large fraction of their time running sequentially through character buffers. These are array elements, again, but here programmers usually access them indirectly through local pointers. The dominant operations are not arithmetic any more -- they are tests or comparisons for branching and mere copying.

Finally, we analyzed a program for CAD of IC's, which manipulates a nontrivial dynamic data structure. The fields of a few nodes (structures) are accessed several times indirectly through local pointers, before the program shifts its attention to some other nodes linked to the previous ones. Again, we found high frequencies of test/compare-&-branch and of copying.

In all cases, we saw that programs are organized in procedures and that procedure calls are frequent and costly in terms of execution time. Procedures usually have a few arguments and local variables, most of which are scalars, and are heavily used. The nesting depth fluctuates within narrow ranges for long periods of time.

We found low-level parallelism although usually in small amounts, mainly between address and data computations. The frequent occurrence of conditional-branch instructions greatly limits its exploitation.

General-purpose computations, as usually expressed in von Neumann languages, are carried out by walking through static or dynamic data structures in some - usually regular - path. Operand addressing, copying, and comparing for decision making, are factors of prime importance. Procedures are heavily used for hierarchical organizations. Numeric computations are frequent and expensive in some applications.

In the next chapters, possible architectural features for exploiting these program characteristics will be presented.

Chapter 3

The RISC I & II
Architecture and Pipeline

In chapter 1 the complexity-speed trade-off was discussed, and the importance of effective utilization of hardware resources was stressed. In chapter 2 we observed the predominance of operand addressing and accessing, of comparisons, and of conditional branching in general-purpose computations.

In this chapter the architecture, the pipeline, and the basic timing of RISC I and II are presented. Architecture and micro-architecture discussions are intermixed because an understanding of the implementation is essential in making architectural decisions that lead to a high-performance processor. It is shown how the RISC I & II architecture efficiently supports integer general-purpose computations with a reduced instruction set, allowing for compact and fast implementation. Benchmark measurements of RISC's performance are reviewed.

The next two chapters deal with the design, layout, debugging, and testing of RISC II, while chapter 6 discusses possible hardware enhancements to RISC-style processors, for increased performance. A detailed and exact description of the RISC II architecture - for reference purposes - can be found in Appendix A.

3.1 The RISC I & II Instruction Set

The architecture of the Berkeley RISC is register-oriented, because program measurements indicate that supporting fast operand accesses is of utmost importance. On the one hand, the compiler by default allocates some frequently used program variables into registers. On the other hand, operations onto operands in memory are decomposed into their orthogonal subtasks of first bringing the operands into registers, then performing the operation, and last moving the result to memory. This decomposition brings no loss in performance when proper pipelining is utilized, while it simplifies the instruction set and its implementation.

All RISC instructions have a fixed width of one word for simplicity and efficiency of the instruction fetch-and-sequence mechanism. The instruction format is simple, with fields at fixed locations, for simple and fast instruction decoding. The operations performed by the instructions all fit within the same general framework, allowing for a simple and fast data-path, for high utilization of the data-path resources, and for a simple homogeneous timing scheme.

RISC is a 32-bit architecture, since a 4 Giga-Byte virtual-address space is believed to be enough for the next several years. Bytes, half-words, and full-word integers (32 bits) are supported in memory; they are all converted into full-words when moved into registers. This offers simplicity, while maintaining full operational flexibility with integers and characters.

This section describes and discusses the RISC instruction set, but does not rigorously define it. Refer to Appendix A for an exact definition.

3.1.1 Register-Oriented Organization

From one point of view, a computer does 70% operand accesses and 30% operations: for each operation one or two source operands are required, and the result is placed into another operand. When one also considers the high frequency of A-gets-B type assignments (§ 2.2.1 [Tane78], [AlWo75]; beginning of sect. 2.3; sect. 2.4), where there are operand references but no operation, one realizes how important it is for a computer system to have quick access to operands. The fastest storage device is a CPU register, not only because the register file is physically small and on the same chip as the CPU, but also because addressing is made with a much shorter address than for cache or memory. For these reasons,

RISC tries to keep as many of its operands as possible in registers. It is not enough to keep only temporary unnamed results in the registers, because expressions are usually very short (see above references), and hence there are not too many such intermediate results. The latter is also the reason why an expression-evaluation stack and a stack architecture were not chosen for RISC. The Berkeley RISC architecture has many registers, organized in multiple overlapping windows, and its compiler by default allocates scalar arguments and local variables of procedures in them. Multi-window register files will be discussed further in sections 3.2, 6.1, and 6.2.

In RISC I and II, operations are performed by 3-operand register-to-register instructions:

$$R_d \;\leftarrow\; R_{s1} \; op \; S2$$

Besides variables, immediate constants are also quite important in computations. In sect. 2.2.2 we saw that they account for 15 to 20 % of the operands used. Thus, in the above generic instruction, the second source operand $S2$ can be either a register R_{s2} or an immediate constant *imm* (see sect. 3.1.4). One of the registers, namely R_0, always contains the hardwired constant zero. Writing into it *is* allowed, but will *not* change its value.

The available operations *op* are:

- integer addition (without or with carry),
- integer subtraction (without or with carry),
- integer inverse subtraction $(-R_{s1}+S2)$ (without or with carry),
- bitwise boolean *AND*, *OR*, *Exclusive−Or*,
- shift left-logical, right-logical, or right-arithmetic (all by an arbitrary amount).

All these instructions can optionally set the 4 existing condition codes (CC's). The add/sub instructions assume 32-bit signed 2's-complement operands. However, there are conditions for branching on, which will act as if the operation (comparison) were between unsigned 32-bit quantities. The *with-carry* versions of add/sub can be used for multi-word precision arithmetic. The shift instructions will shift R_{s1} by the amount (0 through 31 bit-positions) specified in the 5 least-significant bits of $S2$. The logical shifts fill the emptied bit positions with zeros, whereas the arithmetic shift-right sign-extends the leading bit. Rotates and arithmetic shift-left are not included, because they do not exist in HLL's. Shifts by arbitrary amounts (more than 1 or 2 bit-positions) are *not* frequent in HLL's. Thus, their inclusion into our instruction set was contrary to the RISC philosophy; section 4.2 will show the negative consequences of this decision.

Several general and frequent operations, which do not appear explicitly in the above list, can readily be synthesized using the options available:

Instruction:	*Method of Synthesizing it:*
move	$R_d \leftarrow R_s + R_0$
increment, decrement	use add with immediate const. of 1, -1
complement	$R_0 - R_s$
negate (**NOT**)	R_s **XOR** (-1)
clear	$R_d \leftarrow R_0 + R_0$
compare, test	use R_0 as R_d , and set condition codes

3.1.2 Memory Accessing, and Addressing Modes

In RISC I & II all arithmetic, logical, and shift instructions operate on registers. Only the *load* and *store* instructions can access operands in memory and move them to/from registers. This simplifies the processor's data-path and control, the instruction format, and the handling of interrupts caused by demand-paging. Related performance issues are discussed in § 3.3.2 and 3.3.3.

Load and store instructions have a single addressing mode:

$$R_d \longleftrightarrow M [R_{s1} + S2]$$

The result of a RISC add instruction is used as effective address for a memory access. This single addressing mode, which matches well with the rest of RISC's instructions, is quite versatile and permits one to synthesize many other addressing modes:

Mode:	HLL usage:	Synthesizing it in RISC:
Absolute (Direct)	global scalar	$M \ [\ R_B + imm\ ]$ (within $\pm 4K$bytes of base R_B)
Reg. indirect	pointer deref. (*p)	$M \ [\ R_p + R_0\ ]$
Indexed	field of struc. (p→field)	$M \ [\ R_p + field\_offs\ ]$
Indexed	linear byte array (a[i])	$M \ [\ R_a + R_i\ ]$ (assume R_a points to the base of a[.])

Notice that the last mode can only be applied to byte arrays and not to arrays of half- or full-words, because no scaling by 2 or 4 is done on $S2$. The lack of such scaling also reduces the range of addresses accessible with the 13-bit $S2$ immediate offset. The reason for this lack is that there is no circuit in RISC I & II for both shifting and adding in one instruction. The modification proposed in section 4.3 would amend this situation.

The RISC II implementation has one notable exception from the above uniform addressing scheme: the second source $S2$ *must* be an immediate constant for store instructions; thus, the last addressing mode in the table cannot be synthesized for store instructions. The reason has to do with implementation. The register file has two ports because all instructions read two source operands from it. A store instruction with a register-$S2$, however, would need to read three registers: R_d, R_{s1}, and $S2$. This could not be accommodated without major penalties for the data-path, neither could R_d be read conveniently at a later time. Since that addressing mode is not important enough to justify such penalties, the feature was left out, in accordance with the RISC concept.

Memory addresses in RISC are byte addresses. Half-word quantities are aligned on half-word boundaries, and full-word quantities on full-word boundaries. Half-words and bytes are always right-adjusted when they are in registers. The load and store instructions have different versions for full-word, half-word, and byte transfers. These versions perform the necessary change in alignment between memory and registers. The store instruction assumes that the memory system is capable of selectively writing into some of the 4 bytes of a word. Different versions of the load instruction exist for bringing signed or unsigned short quantities into registers with sign-extension or zero-filling.

The versatile addressing mode of the memory access instructions is also used for the control-transfer instructions (jump, call, return) in RISC I & II. However, because the Program Counter (PC) is not in the register file, a separate PC-relative addressing mode was added for control transfers:

$$effective\_address \ = \ PC \ + \ imm$$

Once that mode existed for jump/call/return instructions, it required a trivial hardware extension to use it for load and store instructions as well. This was done to allow the generation of relocatable code for separately compiled modules. Global data can be allocated next to the code, and referenced relative to the PC.

However, later this turned out to be a bad idea. One wants to keep code and data separate for allowing shared read-only code-segments, and for being able to have separate instruction and data caches (sect. 6.3, 6.4). PC-relative data accesses also preclude the remote-PC scheme (sect. 6.3). Finally, the use of a linkage editor does not pose any serious problems when the code is not relocatable.

3.1.3 Delayed Control Transfer

The Berkeley RISC architecture was designed with pipelining in mind from the very beginning. In particular, overlapping of instruction fetch and execution was assumed. This pipeline is disrupted by control transfer instructions, such as conditional and unconditional jumps, procedure calls and returns. Figure 3.1.1 shows a control-transfer instruction I_1 being fetched and then executed. During its execution, it computes the address of its potential target and evaluates the condition for conditional branching. Simultaneously, the subsequent instruction I_2 is being fetched. When execution of I_1 has completed, the fetching of its target I_3 can start.

Instead of flushing I_2 from the pipeline, and thus wasting one cycle, RISC employs the *delayed-branch* scheme. In that scheme, the transfer of control to I_3 takes effect with a delay of one instruction. I_2 *is* executed regardless of whether the control-transfer is successful or unsuccessful. Thus, an instruction immediately after a jump/call/return effectively belongs to the block preceding the transfer-instruction. The compiler puts a no-op at that place, while the optimizer tries to move a suitable task to that place. This can be done when the transfer-

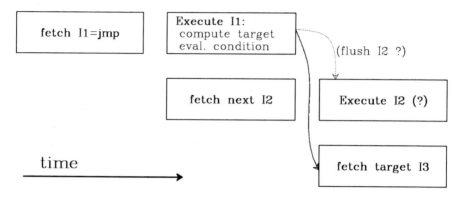

Figure 3.1.1:   Delayed-Branch Scheme.

instruction does not depend on that task.

Measurements have shown [Camp80] that the optimizer is able to remove about 90% of the no-ops following unconditional transfers and 40% to 60% of those following conditional branches. The unconditional and conditional transfer-instructions each represent approximately 10% of all executed instructions (20% total). Thus, while a conventional pipeline would lose $\simeq$20% of the cycles, optimized RISC code only loses about 6% of them. These rough calculations assume that most RISC instructions execute in one cycle (which is not far from true). The above figure agrees with a similar figure given by John Cocke of the IBM Watson Research Center during an informal discussion [Cock83]; the two-cycle branches executed by optimized 801 programs are about 6% of all executed instructions.

For the small fraction of the cycles that the optimizer cannot utilize, an actual no-op instruction has to be inserted at the place of I_2, consuming some code space. The current RISC I & II architectures have no special versions of the transfer-instructions that automatically suspend execution during the next cycle. This choice was made for simplicity. In retrospect, we could have reduced code size by 6% by adding the suspension capability with minimal penalty. The area penalty would be about 0.1% for a circuit that flushes I_2 from the input of the opcode-decoder and replaces it with a no-op. There would be no time penalty because that decoder is still small enough so that it does not affect the critical timing path (§ 4.3.3).

Control-transfer instructions use the same addressing modes as load's and store's. PC-relative is the preferred mode for jumps within a procedure, while register-indexed jumps can be used for table-driven case statements. Call instructions save the value of the PC into a register. The return instruction is register-indexed only; it uses the contents of the register where the corresponding call had saved the PC. In RISC II the return instruction is a conditional one, just like jumps. The usefulness of such instructions is very limited, but their implementation resulted quite naturally. Later, it turned out that conditional returns interfere with the critical path of interrupt assertion because an overflow trap should not occur on an unsuccessful return. This is another case where deviation from the RISC concept led to implementation penalties.

3.1.4 Fixed Instruction Format

An important contribution to processor complexity comes from instruction decoding, and, in particular, from the task of extracting the various instruction fields. RISC I & II have a simple instruction format, with fixed field positions. This led to a very simple and fast decoding circuit (§ 4.3).

All RISC instructions are full-words of 32 bits. This greatly simplifies the instruction fetch and decoding task. Figure 3.1.2 shows the two instruction formats employed. Thirty-two registers are visible to the compiler at any one time, and thus a 5-bit field is necessary for specifying the sources and the destination. There is space for 128 opcodes, although only 39 of them are currently used. One bit (**SCC**) in every instruction can specify the optional setting of the condition codes according to the result (R_d) of the instruction.

The **DEST** field may specify one of two things in both instruction formats, according to the opcode. For conditional control-transfer instructions, its 4 least-significant bits specify the branch-condition (its MS bit is unused). For all other instructions, the **DEST** field specifies the R_d register number.

The short-immediate format is used for all register-to-register instructions and for register-indexed load, store, and control-transfer instructions. The short-SOURCE2 field consists of the 14 bits that are left over after the assignment of

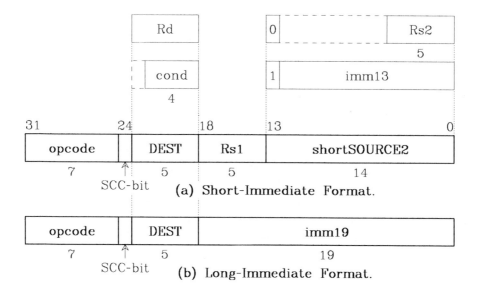

Figure 3.1.2: Instruction Formats.

the other fields. Its leading bit specifies whether it should be interpreted as R_{s2} or as an immediate constant. In the former case, 8 of the 14 bits in the field are discarded (wasted). In the latter case, a 13-bit signed 2's-complement immediate constant is assumed.

The long-immediate format is used for all PC-relative instructions. Since the PC is the first source for them, these instructions need no R_{s1} and can have a wider immediate constant.

This format is also used for the *load-high* instruction, which takes a 19-bit immediate and places it into the 19 high-order bits of R_d, simultaneously zeroing the 13 low-order bits. *Load-high* can be used, in conjunction with the 13-bit immediate field of the following instruction, for loading any arbitrary 32-bit constant into a register. This method of introducing arbitrary constants into registers requires 64 bits of code space and 2 execution cycles. It was preferred over the more complex alternative relying on a single, longer instruction format that could hold the whole 32-bit constant. Since the memory bus is only 32-bits wide, two cycles would still be required for fetching such an instruction; thus there would be no performance gain. The size of that instruction would have to be 64 bits for proper alignment in memory, and no gains in code size would result either. Finally, a PC-relative load instruction can be used for the same purpose, but that means that parts of a code memory segment are read as data (see end of § 3.1.2).

3.1.5 Lack of String, Multiply, Floating-Point Support

RISC I & II have no support for character-string operations, integer multiplications or divisions, or any kind of floating-point operations. There are various reasons for this.

Hardware support of some of these functions requires considerable silicon area, for instance a parallel multiplier, a floating-point unit, or support for more sophisticated string operations. If such a unit were included in the *central* data-path, the basic cycle time would be severely lengthened, due to increased size and capacitance. In § 4.2.4 we will see how even the moderately-sized shifter slows down the basic machine cycle. Another alternative is to place these units *on* the CPU chip, but outside the central data-path. This would make access to them slower than access to the integer adder, but it wouldn't appreciably slow down the other operations.

A third alternative is to place special hardware *off* the CPU chip, for instance as a *co-processor*. Due to chip area limitations, the latter is the most attractive solution for today's technology. According to the views expressed in chapter 6, the integration of functional units such as an instruction cache on the CPU chip is very desirable and has higher priority than the integration of a large arithmetic unit. That means that the co-processor solution will remain attractive during the next few years as well. Co-processor architecture and interfacing is a large and important research area, which could not be undertaken as part of the Berkeley RISC project. For these reasons, RISC I & II have no parallel multiplier or floating-point hardware. Partial support for integer multiplication in the form of one step of Booth's algorithm is a feasible and attractive solution. The main reason why this was not included in RISC I & II is the lack of man-power for their design.

The situation for character string operations is different. These have not yet been standardized in the High-Level-Languages themselves. Most C programs perform them at the lowest character-by-character level (see for example the procedure *gline* in sect. 2.4.2). Pascal does not even have variable-size strings -- it merely has fixed size character arrays. Under these circumstances, it obviously makes no sense for the hardware to support something that the HLL itself does not support. This is, nevertheless, a very interesting area for future research and standardization. It is wasteful, in terms of memory bandwidth, to deal with strings at the character-level. One could decide to align all strings on word boundaries, and mark their end by null-byte padding in the last word (one or more null bytes to fill the word). Co-processors are well suited for supporting string operations as well, since strings are most likely to be kept in memory, and a co-processor hanging off the memory bus can process them as they go by on the bus.

3.2   The RISC I & II Register File,
with Multiple, Overlapping, Fixed-Size Windows

The importance of fast operand accesses and the desirability of keeping as many of them as possible in CPU registers were presented at the beginning of § 3.1. Registers are few in number, and instructions address them directly by their name. For both of these reasons they can only be used to hold scalar variables. One way of deciding which scalars to keep in registers is to rely on hints from the programmer, as are available in the language C. For global variables, this is probably the only way the compiler can know which ones to allocate in registers since programs usually have more global variables than the machine has registers.

But the situation is different for local variables. The measurements of Tanenbaum, and of Halbert and Kessler given in § 2.2.2 show that, for more than 95% of the dynamically called procedures, 12 words of storage are enough for all their arguments and locals. Thus, it is feasible for an architecture to have enough registers so that the compiler can allocate local scalars into registers by default. In case not all of them fit, the compiler will simply place the remaining variables in memory. The decision is not critical since the latter cases are so rare. The measurements from [PaSe82] reported in § 2.2.2 showed that out of 100 HLL operand references, about 20 were to constants, 55 to scalars, and 25 to arrays/structures. We can exclude constants from our count, since they are accessed as part of the instructions themselves. We can also safely assume that for every HLL array/structure reference there is also at least one access to a scalar at the machine level: the array index or pointer to structure. Thus, a more representative ratio ay be: $55+25=80$ scalars accesses versus 25 non-scalar ones. Data from [PaSe82] and from our own measurements reported in § 2.4, indicate that about 80% of the scalar references are to local scalars. Thus, about 60% of all accesses are made to local scalars, and about 40% of them access all other kinds of objects. Since so few words are accessed with such a high frequency and with direct addressing, allocating them into registers is the obvious way of providing fast access to them.

The problem with keeping locals in registers is that they have to be saved on every procedure call and restored from memory on every return. This is the main source of the very high cost of procedure calls in terms of execution time (25 to 40 %, § 2.2.1: [PaSe82] [Lund77]). Argument passing is the second main source of cost. But, while procedure calls occur frequently, roughly once every 8 HLL statements (§ 2.2.1: [AlWo75] [PaSe82] [Tane78]), strong variations of their dynamic nesting depth are rarely observed. This locality of the nesting-depth means that, if sufficient register storage is provided for *a few* activation records, instead of only for one, then register saving and restoring can be reduced dramatically. This led Halbert and Kessler to propose a large register file with multiple overlapping windows for the RISC architecture [HaKe80]. Previous proposals on this subject had been made by R. Sites [Site79], and F. Baskett [Bask78], although their schemes differed from the one used in RISC I & II. Multiple register windows had appeared in processors before RISC, but they were usually intended for multiple processes rather than for procedures, or they had no overlap. More measurements and studies on multiple windows can also be found in [DiML82] and [TaSe83]. The latter paper studies the problem of optimally managing the RISC register file.

3.2.1 Overlapping, Fixed-Size Windows

Figure 3.2.1 (a) shows the organization of a register file into fixed-size, overlapping windows. Not all CPU registers are simultaneously visible by the machine language programmer at any given time. The ones that are visible are called "the current window". The window-number inputs to the decoder select the current window. They are supplied by the CPU state. The register-number inputs to the decoder are supplied by the instruction, and they select one register within the current window. Some registers belong to two windows but have different numbers in each one of them; they are called "overlap registers". Other registers belong to a single window and are called "locals". The scheme works regardless of the numbering sequence in each window, as long as all windows have the same sequence. Figure 3.2.1 (a) shows a small register file with two overlapping windows. In addition, RISC I & II also have some registers, -- called "global" and not shown in fig. 3.2.1 -- which belong to all windows and have the same number in each.

The window number changes every time a procedure call is executed. Thus, every procedure activation record corresponds to a different window (overflows are dealt with in the next sub-section). The compiler allocates the local scalar variables of procedures into the "local" registers, so that no other activation record (window) has access to them. Thus, saving and restoring the registers on call and returns is not necessary. Local non-scalar variables, as well as scalar ones for which there are no registers available, are allocated on the execution stack in main memory, as usual.

The windows are organized in a stack. Parent and child procedure pairs are thus given adjacent, i.e. overlapping, windows. The compiler allocates the scalar arguments of procedures into the "overlap" registers. These registers appear with one fixed numbering to all parent procedures ("outgoing-argument" registers), and with another fixed numbering to all child procedures ("incoming-argument" registers). In preparation for a procedure call, the parent writes the actual arguments into the former registers of the "current" window, and the child has them available in the latter registers of its own window. Thus, the overlap of windows allows for arguments to be passed in registers. These same "overlap" registers are also used for saving the return-PC, and for returning values from child to parent procedure.

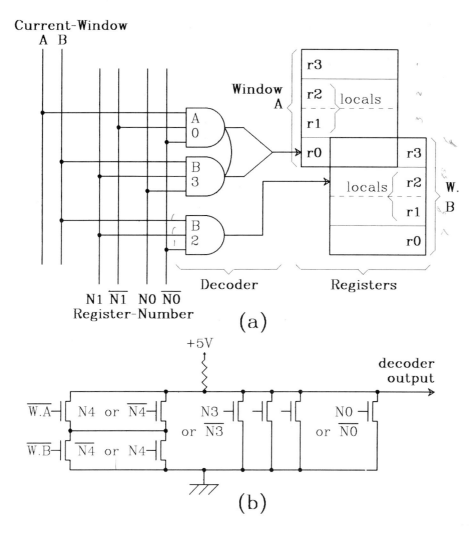

Figure 3.2.1: Overlapping Fixed-Size Windows.

In this scheme windows and overlaps have a fixed size, which allows the simple and fast AND-OR decoding shown in figure 3.2.1 (a) (see sect. 6.2 for a discussion of this point). In RISC I the overlap sections contain 4 registers, the local sections contain 6 registers, and there are 18 global registers. In RISC II overlaps have 6 registers, locals have 10 registers, and there are 10 global registers. The register numbering for RISC II can be found in Appendix A. That numbering is such that overlap registers appear in their two windows with 5-bit numbers that differ in only one bit position. The special NMOS decoder of figure 3.2.1 (b) is then possible, which is significantly faster than the general OR-AND-INVERT decoder. This observation was made *after* RISC II was submitted for fabrication, so the circuit was not used in the actual chip.

3.2.2 Circular-Buffer Organization

The absolute procedure nesting depth is virtually unbounded. The number of register windows physically present in a CPU chip must be not only bounded but also quite small. Locality of nesting-depth refers to the relative depth changes of procedure nesting during a limited time interval, and implies that its fluctuations around a certain depth are fairly small. The CPU register windows are used for the few most recent activation records, for the top of the nesting stack. Older activation records may have to be saved in memory, when the nesting depth increases, and the windows which they occupy need to be re-used for younger procedures. Later on, as the depth decreases, these records have to be restored into the register file windows. The actual organization of the CPU windows is not an infinite stack, but rather a circular buffer for the top of that stack only. The rest of the stack is maintained in memory.

Figure 3.2.2 illustrates the circular-buffer organization. Two pointers are used to keep track of empty and occupied windows. The Current-Window-Pointer (CWP) points to the window of the currently active procedure ("window-number" in fig. 3.2.1). The Saved-Window-Pointer (SWP) identifies the youngest window that has been saved in memory. In the example of figure 3.2.2 a register file consisting of 6 windows is shown, with four of them being currently occupied. For grouping and identification purposes, the overlap registers are shown as belonging to that window in which they constitute input arguments. This grouping is important for the discussions that follow. The variables that are kept in overlap registers are only visible by the child procedure in the

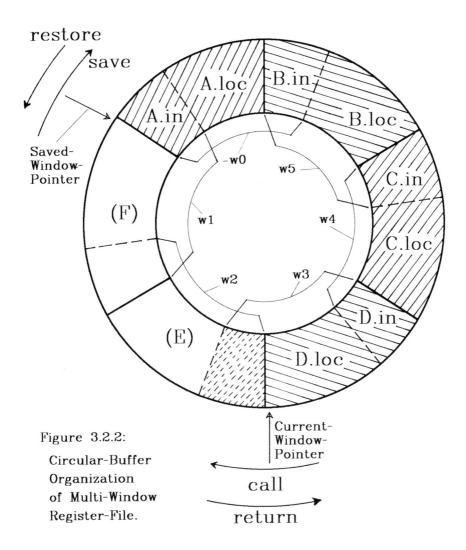

Figure 3.2.2:

Circular-Buffer
Organization
of Multi-Window
Register-File.

High-Level-Language. Only the child has a name for them and can reference them in statements (in languages with up-level addressing, all further descendants can also do so). In contrast, these items are not even variables in the parent procedure, they are merely expression values, and no other statements in that procedure can reference them. This discussion holds true for arguments passed by value or value-return; for arguments passed by reference, the overlap registers actually contain pointers to the arguments.

If procedure D in figure 3.2.2 wants to call a procedure E, it writes the arguments of E in its outgoing-argument registers (in the overlap of w.3 with w.2), and then it executes a call instruction. Call instructions move CWP by one window in one direction (decrement, modulo 6, in our example), while return instructions move it in the opposite direction. If procedure E then decides to further call another procedure F, that call cannot proceed with the current status of window occupancy. The reason is that F could not write into its outgoing-argument area without destroying the input-arguments *A.in* of A. Furthermore, some registers must be kept free at all times for use by the interrupt-handler if an interrupt occurs; these are the locals of w.1 in our case.

At this point, when procedure E executes a call instruction, we say that a *register-file overflow* has occurred. A trap is generated, stopping the call instruction from completing execution. The criterion for the generation of this overflow trap is: *when a call instruction attempts to modify CWP so that it becomes equal to SWP*. The trap gives control to the overflow-handler routine, which saves one or more windows in memory. Tamir and Séquin have concluded that the best strategy, for most practical cases, is to save only one window per overflow trap [TaSe83]. In our example, the overflow-handler will save the areas marked *A.in* and *A.loc* in memory, i.e. only part of w.1, and will then appropriately move SWP to the start of *B.in* .

Similar considerations lead to the criterion for generating the underflow trap: *when a return instruction attempts to modify CWP so that it becomes equal to SWP*. Thus, a single equality comparator circuit is enough for detecting both over- and under- flows.

In summary, an N-window register file can hold only $N-1$ activation records. (In the last table of § 2.2.2, figures were given for $N-1$). Interrupts always modify the CWP in the same way as call's do. So, interrupt-handlers execute in a window where the local registers are guaranteed to be free. Interrupts should not be allowed to nest before the availability of more windows has been checked.

3.2.3 Pointers to Registers

There are cases when a procedure's arguments or local scalars need to be accessed by a pointer or by one of its descendant procedures. The former is true in languages like C, where the programmer is allowed to ask for the address of a scalar variable and to use that address subsequently as a pointer for referencing the variable. That is for example the method for passing return arguments to procedures in C: *scanf("%d %d\n", &i, &j)*. The latter case, references to locals by descendant procedures, appears in languages with up-level addressing, like Pascal. It is usually implemented by maintaining a display of pointers to the bases of the activation records of the (static) ancestors. Thus, this amounts again to accessing a local variable via a pointer.

In this context, there are two methods to allocate local scalars to registers. The first one applies only to languages without up-level addressing. A two-pass compiler is used to recognize the variables which may have aliases and to allocate them in main memory. The second method is to provide means for correctly handling pointers to registers. The RISC architecture specifies the latter approach. There has been a detailed design (data-path and timing) [Kate80] for the implementation of pointers to registers in the RISC I chip, resulting in no lost cycles. However, neither the RISC I nor the RISC II chips have implemented this scheme, because of lack of designer time. The RISC/E design (§ 1.2) does include the handling of pointers to registers. The RISC II micro-computer design contains off-chip circuitry to recognize the use of addresses pointing to registers and to generate an interrupt whenever that occurs [Liou83].

The proposed method for handling pointers to registers in a multi-window environment will be described here in a general form. It was developed in collaboration with D. Patterson, in September 1980.

We use the notion of *"conceptual window stack"*, a conceptual stack in memory consisting of a virtual image of the window frames of all active procedures. It contains one word of storage for each register of each window that has been "called" and did not yet "return". It is similar to the conventional execution stack of procedure activation records, except that RISC uses frames (records) of fixed size. Figure 3.2.3 illustrates this conceptual window stack. For clarity, window frames are shown without their overlap in that figure. The overlap registers are shown as belonging only to the window in which they constitute input arguments, according to the discussion in § 3.2.2. Thus, the "frame

Figure 3.2.3:

Conceptual
Window
Stack.

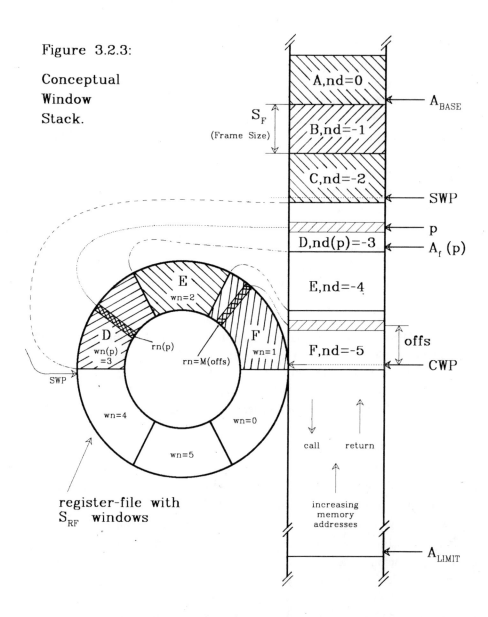

register-file with
S_{RF} windows

size", S_F, shown in that figure is equal to the number of incoming-argument and local registers in one CPU register window, which is also the amount by which the window pointer is moved on each call or return.

All but the top of the conceptual window stack is actually present in memory in the form of older windows saved there, as discussed in § 3.2.2. The top of that stack is in the registers on the CPU. Figure 3.2.3 illustrates this arrangement. The address of a register, at a given time, is the address of the word of the conceptual stack, which it is holding at that particular time.

In what follows, the window stack is assumed to grow towards decreasing addresses. Window frames are uniquely identified by their nesting-depth nd, which is a negative number. That is related to the frame address A_f:

$$A_f = A_{BASE} + nd \cdot S_F \tag{1}$$

where S_F is the size of the window-frame as defined above. The Current-Window-Pointer (CWP) and Saved-Window-Pointer (SWP), which were introduced in the last subsection, are generalized here to be the memory addresses pointing to the same frames as before, but now in the virtual image in the conceptual stack. They thus define the boundaries of the portion of that stack which is currently kept in the register file.

The register file is of size S_{RF} windows, numbered $wn = 0, 1, ..., S_{RF}-1$. By convention, the procedure with $nd=0$ is given the window $wn=0$. Also by convention, each procedure call decrements the current wn, **modulo** S_{RF}. Since each procedure call also decrements the current nd, it follows that the window-number wn of a frame with nesting-depth nd, which is currently in the register file, is:

$$wn = nd \bmod S_{RF} \tag{2}$$

The register-number rn of a register in a CPU window, and the offset, *offs*, of the corresponding word within the conceptual frame, measured from the base of the frame, are related by an arbitrary but fixed one-to-one mapping:

$$rn = M \, (offs) \tag{3}$$

That mapping is defined by the way that the overflow-handler routine saves registers in memory frames, and it may well be a simple linear relation. The compiler must know that mapping in order to generate the address of a local scalar.

The memory address of an argument or local scalar variable which has been allocated into register rn can thus be computed by:

$$CWP + M^{-1}(rn) \qquad\qquad\qquad\qquad (4)$$

where CWP is known at run-time when the procedure is entered.

Now assume that a memory reference is made using a pointer p as effective address. Special action has to be taken if and only if p is pointing to a register:

$$CWP \leq p < SWP \qquad\qquad\qquad\qquad (5)$$

If that last condition holds true, then the window-number $wn(p)$ and the register-number $rn(p)$ of the register where p is pointing to must be determined, so that the memory reference can be correctly turned into a register reference. Let $A_f(p)$ be the base address of the conceptual frame where p is pointing to. Since $0 \leq p - A_f(p) < S_F$, and since $A_f(p) - A_{BASE}$ is a multiple of S_F (by equation (1)), it follows that:

$$\left\lfloor \frac{(p - A_f(p)) + (A_f(p) - A_{BASE})}{S_F} \right\rfloor = \frac{A_f(p) - A_{BASE}}{S_F} \qquad (6)$$

Combining this with equation (1), we get:

$$nd(p) = \left\lfloor \frac{p - A_{BASE}}{S_F} \right\rfloor \qquad\qquad\qquad (7)$$

and combining with equation (2) we find the window-number where p is pointing to:

$$wn(p) = \left\lfloor \frac{p - A_{BASE}}{S_F} \right\rfloor \bmod S_{RF} \qquad\qquad (8)$$

Finally, to get the register-number $rn(p)$, we will use equation (3) and the property $a \bmod b = a - \lfloor a/b \rfloor \cdot b$:

$$rn(p) = M(offs(p)) = M(p - A_f(p)) =$$

$$= M(p - A_{BASE} - nd(p) \cdot S_F) =$$

$$= M\left(p - A_{BASE} - \left\lfloor \frac{p - A_{BASE}}{S_F} \right\rfloor \cdot S_F \right) =$$

$$= M((p - A_{BASE}) \bmod S_F) \qquad\qquad\qquad (9)$$

All this complicated arithmetic reduces to trivial bit-field extractions and concatenations, when the pertinent constants are powers of 2. Such is the case in RISC II:

$$
\begin{array}{lll}
\text{RISC II:} & A_{BASE} & = 2^{32} \\
& S_F & = 64 \ \ (\text{bytes}) \\
& S_{RF} & = 8 \\
& M\ (offs) & = 16 + offs/4 \ \ \ (\text{byte addresses})
\end{array}
$$

Under these circumstances, the important equations become:

$$(Address \ of \ local \ or \ input-argument \ in \ R_n) \ =$$

$$= \ CWP \ + \ (n-16) \cdot 4 \tag{4'}$$

$$wn(p) \ = \ p<8{:}6> \tag{8'}$$

$$rn(p) \ = \ 1\#p<5{:}2> \tag{9'}$$

where $F<m{:}n>$ is the bit-field extraction operator, and $F_1\#F_2$ is the bit-field concatenation operator.

Concerning the detection of pointers p addressing registers, equation (5) says that two full-address comparisons are needed. The comparison of p with SWP is required in order to decide whether p's frame is currently in a register file window or has been saved in memory. The comparison of p with CWP is required in order to decide whether p is pointing into the conceptual window stack or simply to something else in memory. However, this latter condition can also be checked by comparing p against A_{LIMIT} :

$$A_{LIMIT} \ \leq \ p \ < \ SWP \tag{5'}$$

where A_{LIMIT} is the boundary address of the portion of virtual memory allocated for the window stack (see bottom of fig. 3.2.3). If A_{LIMIT} is a "convenient" hardwired constant, then the comparison of p against it may be implemented with very simple hardware. In RISC II, $A_{LIMIT} = 2^{32}{-}2^{24}$, and that comparison reduces to $p<31{:}24>=11111111$, which can be checked with a single NOR gate.

If the window size or register-file size are not powers of 2, then the proposed method is to modify the definitions of S_F and of nd in the following way: S_F

should be defined as the smallest power of 2 that is large enough for a frame to fit in. The *nd* counter, which counts down/up on every call/return, should be made into a conventional counter for its most-significant bits, coupled with a modulo-S_{RF} counter in its least-significant bits. This will waste some words in main memory, where the window stack is kept, but this solution is preferable to implementing hardware to carry out integer divisions by arbitrary constants.

3.3   The RISC I & II Pipelines

The pipeline organizations of RISC I and II are presented here. They form the basis of the micro-architecture of these two implementations, and they have even influenced the original definition of the RISC I & II architecture. RISC I has a two-stage pipeline, while RISC II has three stages. The issue of pipeline suspension during data memory accesses is discussed. Other possible pipeline schemes are reviewed. The default presence of an addition in all register-to-register moves and in all addressing modes of RISC is explained.

3.3.1 Two and Three Stage Pipelines

Most RISC instructions (sect. 3.1) can be executed within the same amount of time, adhering to the following execution pattern:

- read R_{s1} and R_{s2} (or get *PC* or *imm*),
- perform an add/sub or logic or shift operation on $S1$ and $S2$, and
- write the result into R_d, or use it as an *effective-address* for a memory access.

Load and store, the only instructions containing a data memory access, require an additional cycle for completing their execution. They will be discussed in § 3.3.2. The simple execution pattern of the RISC instructions leads to simple pipeline schemes. Figure 3.3.1 shows the RISC I and II pipelines, along with the resulting utilization of the data-path.

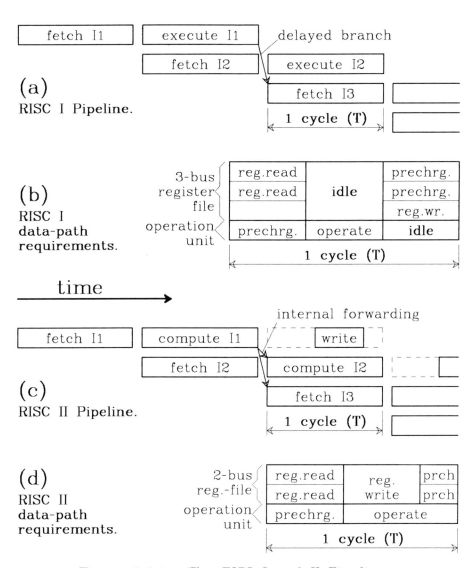

Figure 3.3.1: The RISC I and II Pipelines.

RISC I (fig. 3.3.1(a)) has a simple two-stage pipeline, overlapping instruction fetch and execution, and including the delayed-branch scheme (section 3.1.3). It is assumed that an instruction-fetch memory cycle takes roughly the same amount of time as a CPU read-operate-write cycle. Figure 3.3.1(b) shows the requirements placed on its data-path. For a good performance, a two-port register read is specified, in order to simultaneously get R_{s1} and R_{s2}. Next, the operation is performed onto the two sources, while the register file remains idle. After that one has completed, the result can be written into R_d, while the operational unit, now, remains idle. For an efficient NMOS implementation the two read-busses of the register-file have to be precharged before a read operation is made. In order to reduce the cycle time, RISC I precharges those busses in parallel with writing R_d. Thus, its register file must have 3 busses.

In RISC II a third pipeline stage was introduced (fig. 3.3.1(c)), and the writing of R_d was delayed until that stage. Internal forwarding is used to resolve register interdependencies among subsequent instructions in the pipeline: Two equality comparators detect the conditions $R_{s1,I2} = R_{d,I1}$ or $R_{s2,I2} = R_{d,I1}$. When these occur, the result of $I1$'s operation is automatically forwarded from the temporary latch where it is kept, for use by $I2$, in lieu of the stale contents of $R_{d,I1}$.

The requirements that this pipeline scheme places on the data-path are radically different from the previous ones (figure 3.3.1(d)). Here, the register file is kept busy all the time. It performs the write of $R_{d,I1}$ immediately after the reads of $R_{s1,I2}$, $R_{s2,I2}$. The register-write operation and the precharging of the register-file busses are done in parallel with the ALU or shift operation, instead of sequentially after it as the two-stage pipeline requires. This results in a performance gain, part of which can be spent to perform the precharging *after* the register-writing, thus allowing the use of a two-bus register file. The more compact two-bus register-cell is the main reason why the RISC II chip could pack 75% more registers than RISC I into a 25% smaller area. If an ALU or shift operation takes as much time as a register-write *plus* precharging the register file busses, then precharging the register file busses after the write operation will result in *no* performance loss relative to precharging and writing in parallel, with a three-bus scheme.

3.3.2 Pipeline Suspension during Data Memory Accesses

The RISC I and II CPU chips have a single memory port and assume a non-pipelined memory. This means that only one memory access may be in progress at any time. As a result, when the data memory access of a load or store instruction is being carried out, the rest of the pipeline is temporarily suspended, because an instruction-fetch access cannot be processed at the same time. This situation is illustrated in figure 3.3.2 (a).

The limitation of a single memory port is quite common in microcomputer systems. It is the result of pin constraints, of the presence of a single, non-pipelined memory bank, and of the absence of on-chip cache(s). However, as § 6.3 suggests, it is desirable to integrate an instruction cache on a RISC-style CPU chip, once the technology makes that feasible. An on-chip cache appears as an independent memory port to the CPU, whenever a miss does not occur. The CPU then effectively sees two separate memory ports, one for instructions and one for data. Thus, it is appropriate to study pipelines which are not suspended on data memory references, as figure 3.3.2 (b) shows.

When the constraint of single memory access per cycle is removed, the data access cycle of load and store instructions can occur in parallel with the compute cycle of the next instruction. For store instructions, this poses no problem of data dependency. For load instructions, however, it does. The compute cycle of the instruction immediately following a load must not depend on the value being loaded. This condition needs to be checked by the compiler, which may insert a no-op if no useful work can be done in the slot after the load instruction. Alternatively, such a dependency may be detected by hardware, which then suspends the pipeline while waiting for the data to arrive from memory.

If the register-file can only handle a single register-write per cycle, as in the case of RISC II, a dummy pipeline stage has to be inserted into *all* instructions at the place where loads perform their memory access (figure 3.3.2 (b)).

An advanced pipeline scheme using dual memory write-ports certainly speeds up load and store instructions. But what is their overall impact on performance? How frequent are store instructions, and how frequent are load instructions followed by a computation that doesn't depend on them? John Cocke of the IBM Watson Research Center gave the following numbers regarding the 801 during an informal discussion [Cock83]. About 16% of all executed instructions (on

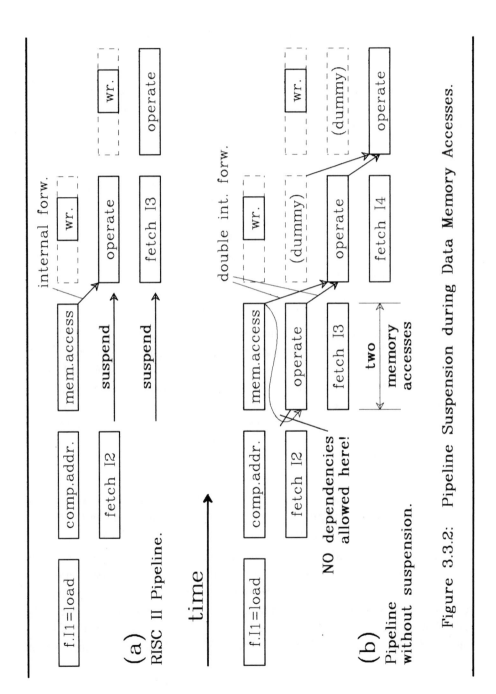

Figure 3.3.2:   Pipeline Suspension during Data Memory Accesses.

the 801) are loads followed by an independent computation, and about 9% of all executed instructions are loads followed by a dependent computation. As far as data memory accesses are concerned, the 801 has a pipeline similar to fig. 3.3.2 (b), but with dual-port register writes and no dummy stages. Cocke gave no figure on the percentage of store instructions, but these usually range around 10% (see e.g. sect. 2.2.1 [AlWo75]). These numbers show that about one quarter of all execution cycles can be saved in the 801 by not suspending the pipeline on data memory accesses.

However, these figures concern a processor with *no register windows.* Such processors need to access variables in memory or save/restore registers more often than processors with register windows. RISC programs execute fewer loads/stores. In three measured program runs, 17%, 13%, and 15%, respectively, of all executed instructions were load's [PaSe81, fig.15]. The corresponding percentages for store instructions were 1%, 1%, and 9%. In RISC, the instructions following the load's can be expected to depend on them more frequently than in other architectures, because restoring multiple registers from memory, upon procedure returns, is much less frequent. Thus, the percentage of RISC execution cycles that can be saved by allowing simultaneous instruction-fetches and data-memory-accesses, can be estimated to be in the range of 10%.

During the RISC design process, another possibility was considered. If no other instruction can be fetched for execution during the data-memory-access cycle, one could try to pack more information into the load/store instruction itself, so that the CPU can do something useful during the above cycle. As an example, a third instruction format could be introduced, where the short-SOURCE2 of figure 3.1.1 would be spit into a 9-bit source-2, $S2$, and a 5-bit R_{s3} specifier. Load and store instructions having this format would perform the following operations during their two execute-cycles:

- $eff\_addr \leftarrow R_{s1} + S2$
- $R_d \longleftrightarrow M[eff\_addr]$; compare-&-set-CC's: $R_{s1} - R_{s3}$

These instructions could be used for implementing combinations of HLL statements such as:

c = *p ;   if (p >= limit) ....

Such combinations are quite rare, however. For example, in the critical loops of section 2.4, there are some program segments in procedure *gline()* of *sed* (2.4.2) that come *close* to the above; however, still *none* of them is suitable for this optimization. In any case, the inclusion of instructions like the above would lengthen the basic processor cycle-time, because additional register-number latches and multiplexors would be required in the critical path of register-number decoding (section 4.2). Thus, such instructions were not included in the RISC architecture.

3.3.3 Other Pipeline Schemes, and the Issue of Default Addition

More pipelining than what RISC II has is possible in RISC-style register-to-register architectures. Figure 3.3.3 compares the 3-stage RISC II pipeline (a), with the 4-stage 801 pipeline (b) [Cock83]. The 4-stage pipeline pushes the data-path utilization as far as data-dependencies permit. The result of an arithmetic, logic, or shift operation may be used as a source for the operation of the next instruction as soon as it becomes available (arrow (1) in fig. 3.3.3(b)). In order to avoid doubly-delayed jumps (arrow (2) in the same figure), the 801 performs the addition of the *PC* with the immediate offset, for PC-relative branches, in parallel with the source-register reads (arrow (3)). Of course, the 4-stage pipeline places heavier requirements on the register file and on the instruction-fetch mechanism. Register reads and writes are performed in the same cycle, and the time to fetch an instruction must be as short as the time to perform an addition. All these issues are studied in more detail and to a greater depth in Robert Sherburne's thesis [Sher84].

In the Berkeley RISC architecture there is no register-to-register *move* instruction. It is synthesized by executing $R_d \leftarrow R_s + 0$, thus performing a dummy ALU or shift operation which by default exists in every RISC instruction. This architectural decision can be explained on the basis of the pipeline organization. In RISC I (fig. 3.3.1(b)), *move* instructions with no ALU/shift operation could execute about 30% faster. However, the corresponding shorter cycles would make timing irregular and introduce significant implementation difficulties. Furthermore, they would require a 30% faster instruction-fetch mechanism, even though this increase in speed could not be exploited during the rest of the cycles. Refering to figure 3.3.3, it can be seen that, in RISC II (a), and in the 4-stage pipeline (b), removing the *op* part from one instruction execution, would yield no performance gain either, as long as the pipeline is limited by instruction-fetches and by register-file accesses. In part (c) of the figure, a

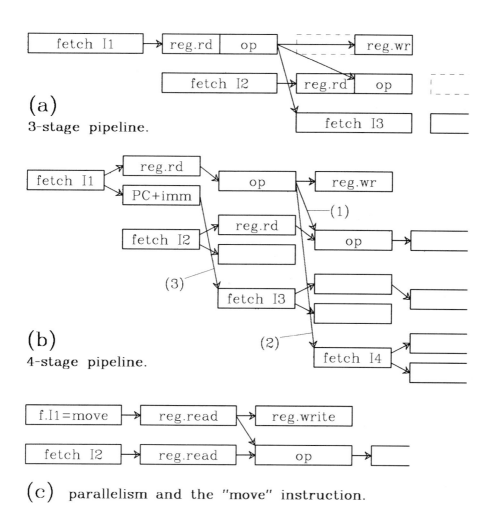

(a)
3-stage pipeline.

(b)
4-stage pipeline.

(c) parallelism and the "move" instruction.

Figure 3.3.3: Various Pipelines.

pipeline is shown which could exploit the available parallelism in the case of a move instruction. Two instructions would have to be fetched and executed simultaneously. The MIPS processor [Henn83] does allow two instructions to be packed in one word and be fetched from memory simultaneously. However, each major execution cycle (pipeline-step) contains two minor cycles. When two register-to-register instructions are packed together, they are in fact executed sequentially -- each during one minor cycle -- because of the lack of sufficient hardware resources to support more parallelism.

Another related issue is the single addressing mode of RISC I & II, which always performs an addition when computing the effective-address, regardless of whether it is needed or not. References such as mere pointer indirections ($*p$) are executed by $R_d \longleftrightarrow M[R_p + 0]$, and the addition is wasted. The reasons for this architectural decision again have to do with the pipeline scheme and with the single memory-port. Figure 3.3.4 (a) shows the execution of a load instruction in the RISC II pipeline. If its address calculation requires no addition, then the data-memory-read operation could be performed half a cycle earlier, as shown in part (b). This would allow the next instruction to start executing one half or even one full cycle earlier. However, the data memory access would have to overlap with the instruction fetch accesses, something which RISC I & II cannot do, as discussed in § 3.3.2. Section 6.4.1 will show how the timing of fig. 3.3.4(b) is possible *including* the addressing addition if a data-cache is used.

Instead of trying to start the memory access and the next instruction earlier than normal, some other useful work could be done in lieu of the unnecessary address addition. Examples of what these modified load/store instructions could do are:

- choice of: $eff\_addr = R_{s1}$, or $eff\_addr = R_{s1} + S2$, and
- optionally compare-&-set-CC's: $R_{s1} \pm S2$, or
- optionally: $R_{s1} \leftarrow R_{s1} + S2$.

The former option of comparing and setting the CC's is similar to the variation that was examined at the end of § 3.3.2. The latter option of modifying R_{s1} is similar to the auto-increment/decrement modes of the PDP-11 and VAX-11 architectures. Shustek [Shus78] found that about 15 % of the statically used addressing modes on the PDP-11 are auto-inc/dec modes, but he also found that some of

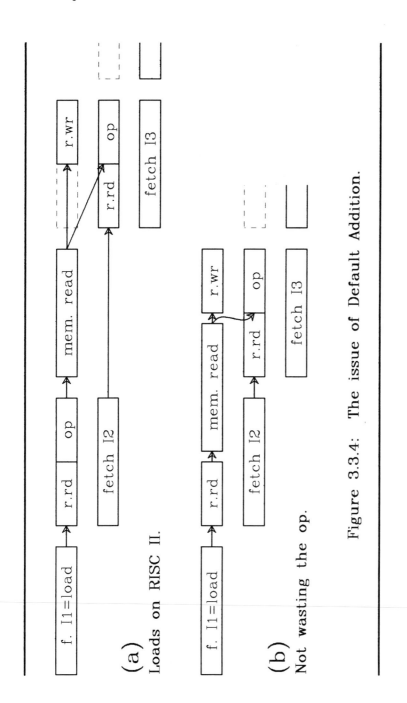

Figure 3.3.4: The issue of Default Addition.

them were merely used to increment/decrement the register without using the accessed memory word. The auto-inc/dec modes are well suited for stack accesses, which the PDP-11 uses a lot because it has few registers (only 32% register-mode usage, in the above study). RISC, on the contrary, performs many fewer memory references, thus the gain which auto-inc/dec mode could bring is limited. Besides, a complication would arise with these modes. Writing into R_{s1} would have to occur during the data-memory-access and if that access leads to a page-fault interrupt, R_{s1} would already have been modified. We preferred not to implement any of those modified load/store instructions, in order to stay with a clean and simple architecture.

3.4   Evaluation of the RISC I & II Instruction Set

In this section we evaluate the Berkeley RISC architecture from various points of view. First, its most controversial part, the reduced instruction set is considered. We discuss its appropriateness for a High-Level-Language (HLL) computer, its impact on code size, and its effect on machine performance. The overall machine is then evaluated, taking into consideration the large multi-window register file, the reduced design time, and the elimination of design errors.

3.4.1 Instruction Set and High-Level-Languages

RISC instructions have some similarity to the micro-instructions on typical micro-programmed machines, some of which will be further discussed in chapter 4:

- All instructions have the same width, and most of their fields have fixed size and position (3.1.4).
- All instructions execute in the same amount of time (except for the "minor" irregularity of pipeline suspension during loads/stores) (3.3).
- All instruction follow a similar and fixed pattern of execution in the data-path (4.1).

- Delayed branches are used (3.1.3).
- The instruction decoder is so simple that it occupies only 0.5% of the chip area (4.4).
- The control signals which sequence the execution of instructions in the data-path are generated by some simple gates that occupy just 1% of the chip area (4.4).

Based on these similarities, some people argue that the RISC instruction set is "of too low a level for a High-Level-Language computer".

However, several frequent HLL statements are compiled into only a single or a few RISC machine instructions. Here are some examples from the critical loop of *fgrep* (§ 2.4.1):

HLL statement:	RISC machine instructions:
if (--ccount<=0)	sub-&-set-CC's: $R_{ccount} \leftarrow R_{ccount} - 1$ jump-if-less-or-equal
c→inp == *p (from the ccomp() macro)	load: $R_{t1} \leftarrow M[R_c + OFFS_{inp}]$ load: $R_{t2} \leftarrow M[R_p + 0]$ sub-&-set-CC's: $R_0 \leftarrow R_{t1} - R_{t2}$
c = c→fail	load: $R_c \leftarrow M[R_c + OFFS_{fail}]$

Thus, RISC machine instructions are not far away from some very frequent HLL statements. We could even argue here that the variants of the load/store instructions which we examined at the end of section 3.3.2 and 3.3.3 actually correspond to *two* HLL statements each.

The topic of High-Level-Language computers (HLLC) has attracted much interest among computer architects and programmers during the last two decades. Some, view a HLLC as a machine that should reduce the "semantic gap" between HLL's and machine code. However, Ditzel and Patterson argue that there is no obvious justification as to why this should be a desirable goal [DiPa80]. Instead, they define a HLLC as one where all programming, debugging, and error reporting takes place in a HLL, so that the user need not be aware of the existence of the machine language. Thus, whether an instruction set is close to micro-code or close to HLL statements is irrelevant to the issue of HLLC. What is important is whether a compiler and a symbolic debugger can be built for a particular architecture, and how fast compiled HLL programs run.

Writing compilers for RISC has proven quite easy, because the instruction set provides simple and straightforward primitives for synthesizing HLL functions. Johnson's Portable C Compiler (PCC) and a peephole optimizer have been modified in less than 6 person-months, to produce code for RISC [Camp80]. Miros also produced another, more solid, C compiler for RISC, again modifying the PCC [Miro82]. This RISC PCC had one third less code-table entries than the comparable VAX-11 PCC.

Other measures can be used to show that RISC is no less a High-Level-Language architecture than are other favorite processors. Campbell [Camp80] gives the static number of machine instructions in 12 C programs, compiled and optimized for the RISC, for the VAX-11, and for the PDP-11. Relative to the VAX-11 code, the PDP-11 code has 40% more instructions, and the RISC code has 67% more instructions, on the average. This shows that, although RISC instructions do contain "less information" than VAX or PDP instructions and could thus be considered "lower level", the difference is not at all that dramatic.

Figure 3.4.1 contains some performance measurements of 5 programs with no procedure calls, published in [PaPi82] and adjusted here for the measured 330nsec and 500nsec cycle times of two scaled versions of RISC II chips (§ 5.2). Execution times of C and Assembly versions of 5 programs are given, normalized relative to the C version on a 500nsec RISC II. We will come back to these performance measurements in § 3.4.3. Of interest here is the ratio of the assembly-code execution-time to the compiled-code execution-time on the various machines. The averages of the corresponding ratios are as follows:

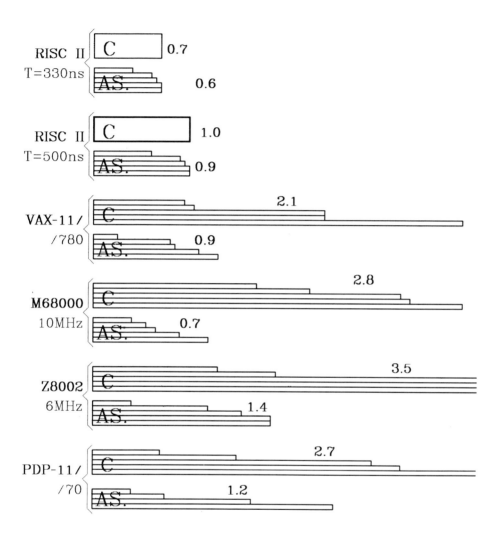

Figure 3.4.1: Normalized execution time of 5 EDN benchmarks (without procedures), on 5 machines, in C and in Assembly.

Machine:	$average \ (\ \dfrac{Assembly\text{-}Code \ \ Exec. \ Time}{Compiled\text{-}Code \ \ Exec. \ Time}\ )$
RISC	0.90 ±0.1
PDP-11/70	0.50 ±0.2
Z8002	0.46 ±0.3
VAX-11/780	0.45 ±0.2
M68000	0.34 ±0.3

This ratio is a measure of the loss in performance due to programming in a HLL rather than in assembly language. The lower this ratio, the more the programmer is tempted to write assembly code. Using this measure, RISC is the best HLL architecture among the ones examined above [PaPi82]. It can be seen that compilers have difficulties to make effective use of the complex instructions that other processors provide.

3.4.2 Instruction Set and Code Compactness

An instruction set and an instruction encoding that achieve compact code are desirable for two main reasons. Firstly, they allow the computer system to have smaller memory devices for holding the same amount of compiled programs. Memory devices, here, are disks, main memory, and (instruction) cache. By being smaller, these devices can be faster and cheaper. Or, alternatively, memory devices of the same size can hold more compiled code. Secondly, when the machine code is more compact, less bandwidth is necessary for fetching instructions into the CPU at the desired rate. This allows busses to be cheaper. Alternatively, the same bandwidth will allow faster fetching -- and thus faster execution -- of the compiled program.

However, in several actual situations, the above effects may be weak, while achieving code compactness may be expensive in other ways. There are two main methods for reducing the average code size. Firstly, an instruction format closer to Huffman encoding may be utilized. This means having a variable number of fields in the instructions, and possibly having the fields encoded with variable sizes. The choices are made according to the relative frequency of usage of instruction and field types. Secondly, frequent sequences of related primitive operations can be made into single instructions. This allows the elimination of fields specifying intermediate results, or of multiple fields specifying common operands. It reduces the number of instructions that need to be fetched.

Instruction encoding and combining must be done carefully, to avoid some possible negative effects on CPU performance and cost. The circuitry that decodes instructions and controls their execution can become large and costly if the instruction encoding is too complicated. Performance can be severely impaired if decoding the instruction must involve *serial* rather than parallel operations. The extraction and interpretation of critical instruction fields should not depend on previous complex decodings of other fields. Also, instructions that require a long execution time, with many intermediate results, may necessitate the inclusion of too many latches into the data-path. This may slow down execution, due to increased capacitive loading, and may render interrupt handling awkward and slow.

Trying to improve performance by compacting the machine code, in order to alleviate the instruction-fetch bottleneck, has its limitations. Firstly, instruction-fetch is usually overlapped with instruction execution, and thus, reducing the instruction-fetch time beyond the available overlap brings no performance gain. Secondly, unless a sophisticated buffering mechanism is used, fetching an instruction takes an amount of time equal to

$$\left\lceil \frac{Instruction\ Width}{Bus\ Width} \right\rceil \cdot (Bus\ Cycle\ Time)$$

In other words, instruction pieces that are narrower than the bus width still require a full cycle to be fetched. Furthermore, instructions of integer word-width may require an additional fetch cycle if they are not aligned on word boundaries. The cost of an instruction-buffering mechanism that could remedy such problems is rarely lower than the cost of simply increasing the width of the bus and of the memory devices, and thus achieving the same fetch rate with wider instructions that are more conveniently aligned.

All these considerations convinced us to stay with the simple instruction set, and with the two fixed and regular instruction formats of section 3.1, even though they are somewhat wasteful in code size. Instructions are word-aligned, and their width is always one word. Thus, exactly one cycle - the minimum possible

- is required to fetch any instruction. The execute-cycle of instructions was defined to perform as much work as practically possible during the one cycle that it takes to fetch the next instruction. As a result of the simple instruction format, the decoding and field-extraction circuitry is trivial, at most 1 or 2 % of the chip area (§ 4.3). The relevant trade-offs were studied carefully, such as long constants (§ 3.1.4) and modified loads/stores (§ 3.3.2 and § 3.3.3). However, in all cases, the simpler solution looked better. After all, memory costs are decreasing, and "wasting" memory is quite common. For example, a full word (32 bits) is usually allocated for every integer, regardless of its actual range.

Even though RISC has such a simple instruction set and instruction format, its average code size is only modestly larger than that of other processors:

Code Size Relative to RISC		
Machine:	Averaged over:	
	11 C programs [PaSe82]	12 C programs [Camp80]
RISC I, II	1.0	1.0
VAX-11/780	0.8 ±0.3	0.67 ±0.05
M68000	0.9 ±0.2	
Z8002	1.2 ±0.6	
PDP-11/70	0.9 ±0.4	0.71 ±0.12
BBN C/70	0.7 ±0.2	

We see that RISC code is usually not more than 50% larger than the rather compact VAX-11 code.

Garrison and VanDyke have studied how much RISC code size could be reduced by encoding the same instruction set with variable-length fields and instructions [GaVD81]. Their results, which are also reported in [Patt83], indicated that the following savings, relative to the present RISC format, are possible:

Huffman encoding (4 to 67 bits/instr.):   43 % savings
8-, 16-, 24-, and 32- bit instructions: 35 % savings
16- and 32- bit instructions: 30 % savings

The last encoding is done by introducing half-word encodings for 7 special cases of existing RISC instructions. This simple encoding certainly brings RISC code size into the same range as code for other popular processors. Patterson et.al. investigated the use of this encoding in connection with the RISC II Instruction-Cache chip [Patt83].

3.4.3 Instruction Set and Machine Performance

Von Neumann computers get high performance either from fast circuit technology or by exploiting fine-grain parallelism. The latter can be achieved in several ways. One is the "special-case" method. Some frequent combinations of primitive operations are detected by the architect and are made into single instructions. Then, the micro-architect tries to implement these instructions in such a way as to exploit the parallelism available among the primitive operations. Another way is the "general-case" method. A data-path with the desired capabilities and cost is conceived first. Next, the architect defines simple instructions that describe the primitive operations available on the data-path. Then the micro-architect undertakes to pipeline these primitive instructions in such a way that they constantly keep all data-path resources busy.

The "special-case" method has the advantage of requiring less instruction-fetches for the same amount of work; it also has the questionable advantage of allowing better exploitation of parallelism since the particular environment of execution is better known. It has the disadvantages of requiring complex control and of only dealing with special cases. The opposite situation holds true for the "general-case" method. It is more flexible to exploit parallelism, wherever it is available, or to expose the machine capabilities and to allow the compiler/optimizer to make full use of them. Controlling the instruction execution is also simpler. Providing reasonable amounts of pipelining is not very hard, even though the previous and subsequent primitive operations are not known (see chapter 4). The "general-case" has the disadvantage of requiring more instruction fetches.

Architectures with complex instruction sets intend to get high performance using the "special-case" method. Reduced instruction set computers follow the "general-case" approach.

The Berkeley RISC experiment has shown that the differences in code size between the two methods need not be large (§ 3.4.2). On the other hand, it has shown that the differences in size and complexity of the control circuitry *is* large. While the control section covers 50 to 60 % of the chip area in the M68000 or in the Z8000, it only covers 6 to 10 % of the RISC I or II chip area (see § 4.4 and [Fitz81]). We believe that it is better to spend hardware resources in implementing an instruction-cache, than to spend them in implementing complicated control circuitry with a big micro-program ROM. The reason is that an instruction-cache holds the instructions that are *dynamically* most frequently used, while micro-storage holds the *statically* most frequent primitives, or -- even worse -- some rarely used complex constructs. In RISC I & II, the scarce chip transistors were spent to implement a multi-window register file, since that one has even higher priority than an instruction cache (see chapter 6).

We mentioned above that the "special-case" method may have the advantage of allowing better exploitation of parallelism because of the built-in knowledge of the particular execution environment. However, the opposite may also be true. Micro-programmers sometimes find it hard to correctly optimize all the instructions in a complex architecture. For example, the VAX-11/780 has an *index* instruction used for calculating the address of an array element, and simultaneously checking whether the index fits within the array bounds. The same task can be performed with multiple simpler VAX-11/780 instructions in 45 % *less* time [PaDi80] ! A similar case for the IBM 370 is reported in [PeSh77]. A sequence of *load* instructions is faster than a *load-multiple* instruction when fewer than 4 registers are loaded.

The Berkeley RISC follows the "general-case" method of pipelining simple instructions. Section 3.3 showed how the memory port is always kept busy and how the register-file and the ALU of RISC II are kept busy all the time except for the cases of dummy additions, when nothing else could practically be done. More hardware resources make possible the exploitation of more parallelism in RISC-style architectures. Such examples were given in 3.3.2 and 3.3.3 for the case of separate instruction and data memory-ports. One can also consider the possibility of simultaneously dispatching multiple simple instructions when multiple functional units exist. Figure 3.3.3(c) offered one such example. A proposal for parallel dispatching and execution of unconditional-branch and of other CPU instructions will be presented in § 6.3.6.

Comparative measurements of RISC II speed, relative to that of other microprocessors and mini-computers, have shown RISC's superior performance [PaPi82] (also in [PaSe82]). For some of the processors, including RISC, these were collected using a simulator. The average performance ratio from those studies is given below, after being adjusted for the cycle times of the actual RISC II chips (§ 5.2):

Machine:	Basic Clock	Reg-to-reg add	$\dfrac{Execution\ Time}{8MHz\ RISC\ Exec.\ Time}$ averaged over 11 programs
RISC II	T=330ns (12MHz)	330ns	0.67
RISC II	T=500ns (8MHz)	500ns	1.00
VAX-11/780	5MHz	400ns	1.7 ±0.9
PDP-11/70	7.5MHz	500ns	2.1 ±1.2
M68000	10MHz	400ns	2.8 ±1.4
BBN C/70	6.7MHz		3.2 ±2.2
Z8002	6MHz	700ns	3.3 ±1.3

Five of the above benchmark programs do *not* have procedure calls, they consist of one single function. The execution-time ratio for these programs was given in figure 3.4.1. They show that the performance advantage of RISC is still present, even when the multiple windows of the register file are not used.

More extensive performance measurements were carried out by Miros [Miro82]. He ran the VAX C compiler on both the RISC simulator and on the VAX-11/780. The compilation of three programs took 26 seconds on a 330ns RISC II (simulated), 38 seconds on a 500ns RISC II (simulated), and 50 seconds on the VAX-11/780. It is worth noting that a register-to-register integer addition takes 330ns or 500ns on RISC II, while the VAX-11/780 data-path can perform such an operation in one 200ns *micro*-instruction, even though the execution of a register-to-register add *instruction* takes 400ns on the VAX-11/780.

3.4.4 Overall Evaluation of RISC I & II

An overall evaluation of the Berkeley RISC architecture must include the multi-window register scheme, the area and transistor statistics of the VLSI implementation, and the human effort that was required to design, layout, and debug the chips.

The evaluation of the multi-window register file was done by Halbert and Kessler and was reviewed in section 2.2.2 (with some further discussion in section 3.2). Here are two more measurements from [PaSe82] for illustration purposes:

Data-Memory-Traffic due to Call's and Return's:		
	PUZZLE	QUICKSORT
VAX-11/780:		
words	440 K	700 K
% of all data-mem-ref.	28%	50%
RISC:		
words	8 K	4 K
% of all data-mem-ref.	0.8%	1%

These numbers only concern the data traffic due to calls and returns. Further savings in memory accesses are achieved by the default allocation of locals into registers. Thus, one realizes the dramatic savings in memory traffic that the multi-window register file provides. Section 6.1 compares register files to cache memories, while section 6.2 examines other possible organizations for them. A study of the trade-off between the size of such a register file and its delays due to capacitive loading can be found in Sherburne's thesis [Sher84].

In the RISC I and II NMOS microprocessor chips, the traditional allocation of scarce silicon resources has been radically altered owing to the reduced instruction set. Control circuitry has been drastically reduced, and the silicon area and transistors saved were used for the large register file. The foregoing evaluation showed how the reduced instruction set leads to high utilization of the data-path hardware by the executing programs. This effect is amplified by the faster basic cycle that a simple data-path achieves, as chapter 4 will show. The multi-window register file further enhances performance. The overall result is what we consider to be the most effective utilization of the scarce VLSI resources for performing general-purpose computations. And, last but not least, the human effort required to design, layout, and debug the processor has been reduced by almost an order of magnitude relative to that required for the design of other microprocessors (sect. 4.5). This reduces costs and allows faster exploitation of new and rapidly changing technologies.

We believe that these points prove the viability of Reduced Instruction Set Computer architectures for general-purpose VLSI processors.

Chapter 4

The RISC II Design and Layout

This chapter deals with the micro-architecture of the RISC II chip. After a detailed description of the data-path (§ 4.1), it presents the fundamental timing dependencies and the particular timing scheme chosen (§ 4.2) as well as the organization of control (§ 4.3) and some design metrics (§ 4.4). The estimates and the rationale which guided the major decisions are discussed and compared with the picture that emerged after the circuit was designed and laid-out.

4.1 The RISC II Data-Path, and its Use for Instruction Execution

This section presents the RISC II data-path and the basic trade-offs which were considered during its design. The general form of the data-path is a direct consequence of the instruction set (sect. 3.1) and of the chosen pipeline scheme presented in section 3.3.

A very compact register cell was essential for the implementation of a large register file. Robert Sherburne designed and laid-out such a compact 2-bus register cell by modifying the classical 6-transistor static cell [SKPS82], [Sher84]. The modification allows dual-port read-accesses with single-bus signal-sensing, but requires both busses for a write operation. Dual read-ports and a single write-port perfectly match the basic RISC instruction pattern of reading two registers R_{s1} and R_{s2}, and writing the result into a register R_d. The cell requires a precharge - read - write cycle, which guided us in the choice of the pipeline scheme (figure 3.3.1(c,d)). This cell is about 2.5 times smaller than the 3-bus RISC I register cell, and this feature constituted the main driving force for the development of RISC II.

An arbitrary-amount bidirectional shifter is included in the data-path, as the instruction set specifies. This was designed and laid-out by the present author. It consists of a cross-bar switch made out of pass-transistors [SKPS82]. A compact and versatile lay-out was achieved by routing one data-bus, R, in the horizontal direction, while the other one, L, is diagonal, thus providing connection points both on the side and at the top of the shifter module; the control-bus is vertical. The elementary shifter cell is a bi-directional pass-gate that is used in one direction for a left-shift, and in the other direction for a right-shift. The shifter busses need to be precharged before they are used.

A 32-bit integer add/sub ALU, the Program-Counter circuitry, and a pipeline latch complement the basic data-path.

4.1.1 The RISC II Data-Path

Figure 4.1.1 presents the RISC II data-path. Its basic parts, namely latches, functional units, and busses are the following:

- *Register File:* 138-word by 32-bit register file, with its dual-port address decoder and with latches *RA*, *RB*, *RD* holding the register addresses (numbers) from the instruction. R_0 is hardwired to contain zero.

- *PSW:* 13-bit Processor Status Word. It includes the *CWP* and *SWP* (sect. 3.2), the condition codes (*CCs*), and interrupt and system control bits (Appendix A).

- *DST:* the Destination latch, serving as the temporary pipeline latch. The result of each cycle's operation is kept in there, until that result is written into the register file, or otherwise used, during the next cycle.

- *SRC:* Input (Source) latch for the shifter. *DST* or *BI* are used as the shifter's output latch.

- *Shifter:* The 32-bit cross-bar shifter. The amount of shifting (0 through 31) is specified by the contents of the *SHam* latch and decoded by the shift-amount decoder (S.DEC). A right-to-left shifting occurs when information flows in the *busR→busL* direction, and a left-to-right shifting for the opposite direction.

- *AI, BI:* the two input latches of the ALU. The ALU has no output latch; it uses *DST* or *busOUT* for that purpose (*busOUT* will dynamically hold information).

- *ALU:* a 32-bit integer arithmetic and logic unit. It may perform addition, subtraction, bitwise *AND*, *OR*, *XOR*, or pass *BI* to the output.

- *BAR:* the Byte-Address Register, which computes and holds the 2 least-significant bits of the sum of *AI* and *BI*. In those cases when the ALU is computing an effective-address, *BAR* will contain the part of the address which specifies the byte-within-the-word alignment.

- *NXTPC:* the Next-Program-Counter register, which holds the address of the instruction being fetched during the current cycle.

- *INC:* an incrementer, which computes *NXTPC* +4 (byte addresses).

- *PC:* the Program-Counter register, which holds the address of the instruction being executed during the current cycle.

- *LSTPC:* the Last-PC register, which holds the address of the instruction last executed - or last attempted to be executed. When an interrupt occurs, *LSTPC* will hold the address of the interrupted (aborted) instruction during the first cycle after the interrupt.

- *IMM:* the Immediate latch to hold the 19 LS-bits of the incoming instruction, which contain its immediate constant (if it has one).

- *DIMM:* the Data.In/Immediate combined latch, preceded by the sign-extender/zero-filler. It holds data coming-in from memory, or immediate operands being forwarded to the data-path.

- *OP:* the 7-bit opcode of the instruction, and the SCC and use-immediate bits of the instruction (bits <31:25>, <24>, and <13> respectively; see fig. 3.1.1).

- *busA, busB:* the register-file busses.

- *busD:* the bus used for feeding *AI*, and for feeding *DST* from the right-hand side of the data-path.

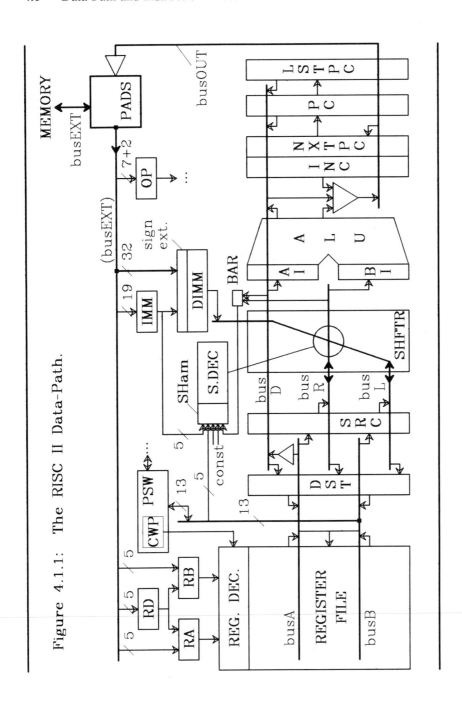

Figure 4.1.1: The RISC II Data-Path.

- *busR, busL:* the shifter's busses, optionally connected by the bi-directional cross-bar shifter. *BusR* is also used for feeding *BI*, while *busL* is also used for introducing *Data.In* and immediate constants into the data-path.

- *busOUT:* the bus used for routing addresses and data to the pads, and form there to memory.

- *busEXT:* The off-chip bi-directional time-multiplexed address/data bus, which connects the CPU to the memory. It is electrically identical with the 32 address/data bonding-pads, and with the 32 wires running in the chip, and feeding *RA*, *RB*, *RD*, *IMM*, *DIMM*, and *OP*.

The next subsection explains how these latches, functional units, and busses are used for executing the instructions.

4.1.2 Paths Followed for Instruction Execution

There are few categories of activities that may be going on in the data-path during each cycle:

- The appropriate two sources $S1$ and $S2$ are routed to the ALU or to the shifter.

- The output of the ALU, of the Shifter, or of the *PC* is routed to *DST*, and is written into its final destination in the next cycle.

- Addresses or data are routed to memory and/or to the *PC* s.

Figure 4.1.2 illustrates how the appropriate two sources $S1$ and $S2$ are routed to the ALU inputs *AI* and *BI*. $S1$ may be a register, or it may be *PC* for PC-relative addressing. $S2$ may be a register or an immediate constant, or it may be *PSW* for the *getpsw* instruction.

Registers R_{s1} and R_{s2} are read through busses *A* and *B*. In case a data-dependency with the previous instruction is detected, internal forwarding occurs (sect. 3.3.1); the *DST* places its contents onto *busA* and/or *busB*. On *getpsw* instruction, reading from the register file is disabled and *busB* is driven from the *PSW*.

Figure 4.1.2:   Paths leading to the ALU.

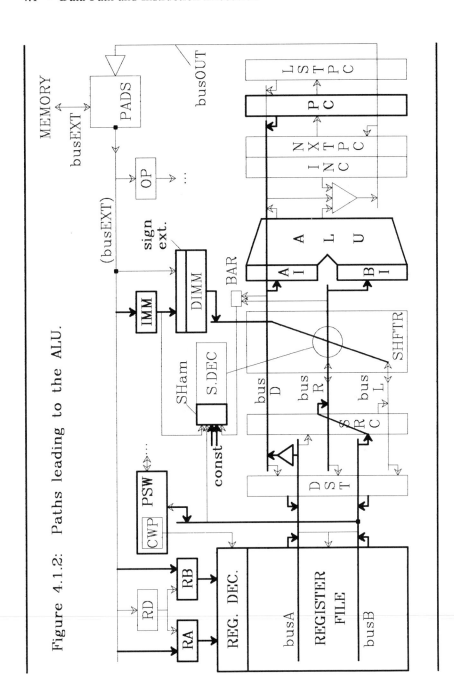

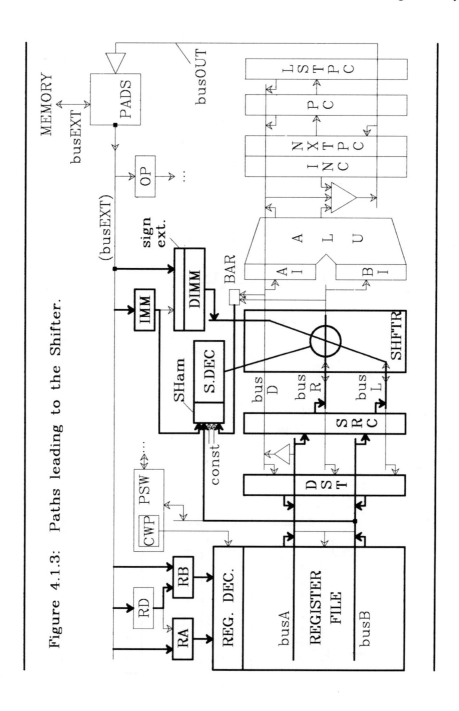

Figure 4.1.3:   Paths leading to the Shifter.

The first input of the ALU, *AI*, is loaded from *busD*. That bus is driven by *PC* or from *busA*, depending on whether a PC-relative or a normal instruction is being executed. The *BI* input of the ALU is loaded from *busR*. That bus is driven from *busB* - through *SRC* - when *S2* is a register or the *PSW*. In that case, the transistors of the shifter are all turned-off, so that *busR* is disconnected from *busL*. When *S2* is an immediate constant, *busR* is fed from *DIMM*, through *busL* and through the shifter. The 19-bit *IMM* latch is connected to *DIMM* in such a way that it feeds the 19 MS-bits of *DIMM*, while the 13 LS-bits of *DIMM* are loaded with zeros. When the instruction contains a 13-bit immediate, the sign-extender converts that into 19 bits. When this MS-aligned 19-bit immediate goes through the shifter, it either stays MS-aligned for *load–high* instructions, or it is right-shifted by 13 and sign-extended (i.e. LS-aligned), for all other instructions.

Figure 4.1.3 illustrates how the appropriate sources are routed to the Shifter. For shift instructions, the quantity to be shifted is R_{s1}, which is read via *busA* and placed into *SRC*. *SRC* then drives *busR* for right-to-left shifting, or *busL* for left-to-right shifting. The amount of shifting is *S2*, a register or an immediate constant. Thus, *SHam* is loaded with the 5 LS-bits of *IMM* or of *busB* which carries R_{s2}.

Alternatively, the quantity to be shifted may be data to or from memory, requiring alignment. In that case, the amount of shifting (alignment) is specified by the *BAR*. When data *from* memory must be aligned at the end of a *load* instruction, *DIMM* serves as the shifter's input. Notice that alignment of incoming data requires *left-to-right* shifting only. When data *to* memory must be aligned during a *store* instruction, that data comes from R_d and is read through *busB* and placed into *SRC*. As it was discussed in section 3.1.2, RISC II limits the addressing modes of *store* instructions to having an immediate *S2*, so that *busB* of the register file can be used to read the data at the same time when *busA* is used to read the index register R_{s1}, and when *busL* and *busR* are used to bring the immediate to *BI*.

Figure 4.1.4 illustrates how the output of the ALU or Shifter, or the *PC*s are routed to *DST*, and later written into their final destination. This final destination for most instructions is R_d, and the *PSW* for the *putpsw* instruction. Data to be written into those destinations may originate from:

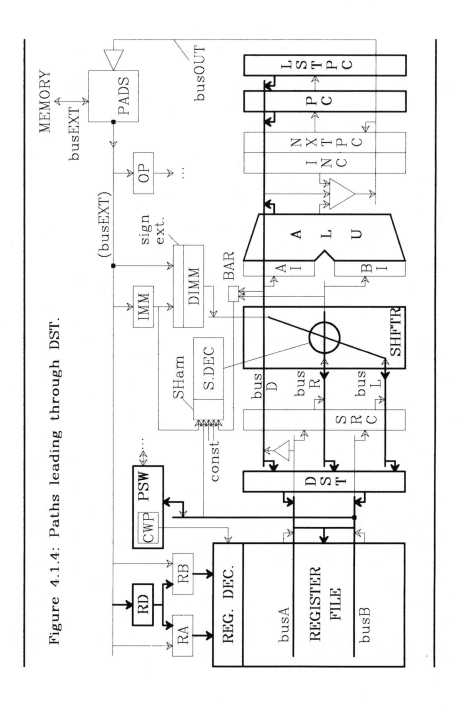

Figure 4.1.4: Paths leading through DST.

- the ALU, for arithmetic and logical instructions, or for the *putpsw*, *getpsw*, and *load–high* instructions. The last two instructions use the ALU in the mode where *BI* is passed intact to the output.

- the Shifter, for *shift* or *load* instructions.

- the *PC*, for *call* instructions, which save their address into R_d for use by the *return* instruction.

- the *LSTPC*, for the *calli* and *getlpc* instructions; these are used on interrupts, in order to get the addresses of the interrupted instruction and of the instruction that was being fetched when the interrupt occurred.

BusD is used to route the ALU output, *PC*, or *LSTPC* into *DST*. The output of the shifter comes from *busR* or *busL*, depending on whether it was a right or left shift, respectively. *DST* holds those results of execution, until the appropriate time in the last pipeline stage when they are written into R_d or into *PSW*. That occurs via busses *A* and *B*.

Figure 4.1.5 illustrates how addresses and data are routed to memory and how the three *PC* registers work. *BusOUT* is the only bus used for sending information out of the data-path, and it is driven by a multiplexor with dynamic storage capability. Addresses for instruction-fetching come from the ALU output in the cases of a successful transfer of control, and from the NXTPC-incrementer in all other cases. The *NXTPC* is always loaded from *busOUT*, with whatever address is sent to memory for instruction-fetching. The *PC* and *LSTPC* registers follow the contents of *NXTPC* with a delay of 1 and 2 pipeline stages, respectively. During data-memory-access cycles, the whole PC-related circuitry freezes (see sect. 3.3.2 on pipeline suspension).

Addresses for data-memory-accesses always come out of the ALU. Data are sent to memory during *store* instructions. After these data have been read from R_d and aligned (fig. 4.1.3), they are temporarily kept in *DST* (fig. 4.1.4). Then, *DST* places them on *busA*, which then drives *busD*, and from which they are put onto *busOUT* (figure 4.1.4).

This completes the description of the paths used for the various CPU activities. The complete execution of an instruction is, in general, a combination of some transfer from figure 4.1.2 or 4.1.3, followed by some operation, followed by some transfer from figure 4.1.4 and some from 4.1.5.

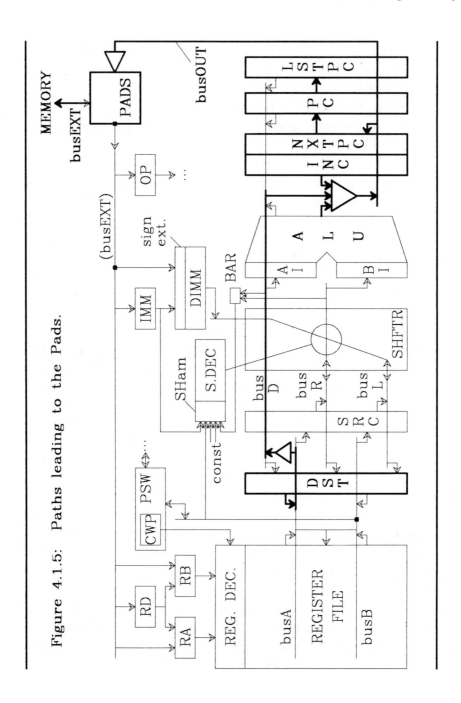

Figure 4.1.5: Paths leading to the Pads.

4.1.3 Trade-offs Considered during the Data-Path Design

To a large extent the RISC II data-path is a direct consequence of the register-cell used, of the pipeline scheme, and of the instruction set requirements. Some of its important characteristics, however, could be different. Here, we will mention some alternatives, and we will give the reasons for our particular choice. These choices will be evaluated in the next two sections. For a more extensive and detailed study of data-path design trade-offs, and one that particularly addresses electrical design issues, refer to Sherburne's thesis [Sher84].

One trade-off relates to the way immediate constants are brought into the data-path. The shifter is also used for that purpose, in addition to its main function of executing shift instructions and aligning the data on load/store instructions. Shift instructions and data alignment match well with each other, because at most one of these operations occurs in any one cycle, and because both occur near the end of the cycle. However, the routing of the immediates does not match so well with those operations, because it has to occur at the beginning of the cycle, and because it may occur in the same or adjacent cycle with one of the other two functions. In spite of that non-optimal match, a timing solution was found and implemented in RISC II (§ 4.2.2). As a consequence of routing immediates through the shifter, the latter was placed between the ALU and the register file.

There are two possible alternatives to the above scheme. Immediates could be brought into the data-path from the right-hand side, using an extra horizontal bus. This would increase the number of busses crossing the PCs and the ALU, which would cause severe problems for the layout of those densely populated areas. Otherwise, immediates could be brought in with an extra vertical bus just on the left-hand side of the ALU. Aligning the immediate to the LS or MS word-position could then be done with a 2-way multiplexor at the input of BI. This solution is feasible, but it was not chosen because it requires the extra space for a 19-bit vertical bus. The horizontal length of the data-path is severly limited by the desire to have 138 registers, in a chip limited in length by the size of the package cavity.

Another trade-off relates to the way the ALU inputs are fed. In the chosen scheme, multiplexing the ALU sources occurs on the busses which feed AI and BI. In this way, the ALU inputs are simple latches, and the register-file busses A and B do not have to extend all the way up to the ALU inputs. This latter fact is advantageous because it reduces bus capacitance thereby speeding-up register-reads. It also alleviates the heavy bus congestion in the *SRC* area. The alternative would be to make the ALU inputs into latches with multiplexors and to extend various busses all the way to them. This scheme would allow registers to be routed directly to the ALU without incurring the extra delay due to the forwarding from one bus onto another. However, it has all the disadvantages corresponding to the advantages of the chosen scheme.

4.2   The RISC II Timing

This section is concerned with the timing of the RISC II data-path. It starts with a discussion of the fundamental timing dependencies, as implied by the instruction set and the pipeline scheme, regardless of a specific data-path. Then, it proceeds to examine how this timing was cast into specific clock phases for the particular data-path that was chosen (sect. 4.1). Finally, the timing picture that emerged after the data-path was laid-out is presented. Discrepancies between the three above timing schemes are discussed and explained, and some conclusions are drawn.

4.2.1 Fundamental Timing Dependencies

Figure 4.2.1 is an abstract timing-dependency graph for the RISC II pipeline (sect. 3.3.). Arrows represent data-path activities, while vertices represent cause-effect dependencies. If an activity Y depends on an activity X and *must* follow it in time, then the arrow representing Y starts from the endpoint of arrow X.

The diagram shown in fig. 4.2.1 assumes no knowledge about the data-path, other than the use of a register file with two read-ports, one write-port, and requiring a precharge - read - write cycle. One counter-clockwise revolution around the top half of the diagram represents the main activities occurring inside the CPU during one machine cycle. Equivalently, one clockwise revolution around the bottom half represents the memory cycle occurring in parallel.

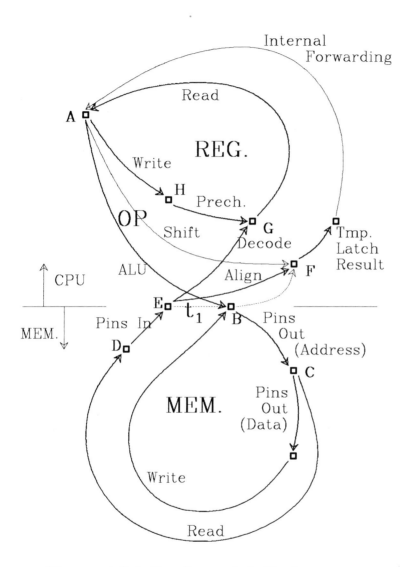

Figure 4.2.1: Fundamental Timing
Dependencies in RISC II.

Point A illustrates that an ALU or Shift operation can only begin after its source-registers have been read, and that a register-write can only begin after the read operation has been completed. Point B shows that the result of an ALU operation can be used as an effective memory address for a data access or for an instruction fetch. Points C, D, E illustrate a memory read. When this is an instruction fetch, then the path E→G shows that the source-register-number fields of the instruction must be decoded before the corresponding register read accesses can start. The path E→F stands for the alignment and sign-extension/zero-filling needed when bytes and short-words are loaded from an arbitrary memory location into the least-significant position of a register. Thus, point F represents the result of the second-to-last pipe-stage, which is to be written into the destination register during the last pipe-stage (point A). The precharge - read - write register-cycle is shown as cycle H→G→A→H.

Figure 4.2.1 has been drawn with some crude notion of actual time durations in it. The length of the arrows is roughly proportional to the delay of the corresponding data-path activities. Not included is an estimate of the routing delays from one functional unit to another, because no specific data-path is assumed at this point. The diagram shows points E and B separated by an *arbitrary* amount of time t_1. Point E represents the end of a memory-read cycle, and point B represents the beginning of the next memory cycle. Because of the multiplexed address/data pins and because of the non-overlapped memory accesses, point B must be *after* point E, and thus t_1 must be >0. Within that constraint, t_1 is an arbitrary design parameter that specifies how much the memory access time (B→C→D→E) is shorter than the overall system cycle time.

The diagram shows quite clearly that the internal-forwarding path, F→A, is not critical. The critical paths lie in the register file loop:

$$(precharge)_{HG} \rightarrow (read)_{GA} \rightarrow (write)_{AH}$$

and the figure-8-shaped path:

$$(decode-register)_{EG} \rightarrow (read-register)_{GA} \rightarrow$$
$$\rightarrow (compute-address)_{AB} \rightarrow (send-it-off-chip)_{BC} \rightarrow$$
$$\rightarrow (fetch-instruction)_{CD} \rightarrow (bring-it-on-chip)_{DE}$$

Thus, using T_{cycle} for the cycle time, we derive the basic critical path equations:

$$T_{cycle} \geq (reg-prech.)_{HG} + (reg-read)_{GA} + (reg-write)_{AH}$$

$$T_{cycle} \geq (reg-decode)_{EG} + (reg-read)_{GA} + (ALU-add)_{AB} - t_1$$

$$T_{cycle} \geq (pins-out)_{BC} + (mem-read)_{CD} + (pins-in)_{DE} + t_1$$

Thus, the parameter t_1 represents a trade-off between memory and CPU speed. The faster the memory-access time is, the larger t_1 becomes, and the slower the register-decoding and reading and the ALU can be.

4.2.2 The RISC II 4-Phase Timing

Mapping a timing dependency diagram, like the one of figure 4.2.1, into concrete clock phases for an actual data-path, requires time-area trade-offs to be considered and compromises to be made. For RISC II, a 4-phase clock was chosen, for the following reasons:

- symmetric clock phases are easy to generate;
- register file operation is non-ideal, due to the high resistivity of the polysilicon word lines;
- the register address decoders are simplified;
- the shifter must be used twice per cycle.

Below, we discuss these points and present the utilization of the data-path during the four non-overlapping clock phases. The choices described here were made before the data-path was laid-out and were based on estimates of the various delays. The next subsection, 4.2.3, compares these estimates with the timing picture that emerged after the lay-out was completed and circuits were simulated with their actual parasitic capacitances.

The timing design started with the estimate that a register read takes more time than a register write, which, in turn, takes more time than precharging the register-file busses. Instead of allocating three unequal clock phases for each one of these operations, it was decided to use a 4-phase clock with two long phases ϕ_1 and ϕ_3 ($\approx$ 80ns each), interleaved with two short phases ϕ_2 and ϕ_4 ($\approx$ 60ns each). This would make clock generation easier, since the generator could now have a 2-phase period. Having more clock-phases, of a shorter duration each, is also useful in fine-tuning the timing of the various operations. On the other hand, 4 phases may result in wasted time during the non-overlap periods between clock phases.

To match the register file requirements with the four defined clock phases, register reads were planned to stretch over both ϕ_1 and ϕ_2, while phases 3 and 4 were allocated to the register-write and precharge operations, respectively. The implications of the high resistivity of the polysilicon word lines was studied carefully. The RC time constant of the address lines can easily reach 50ns, causing significant delays between their near and far ends. If a write operation immediately follows a read operation, the read-word-lines may not be fully deactivated by the time writing begins and cause erroneous register file write operations. To avoid this hazard, it was decided to activate the word-line drivers for read accesses during ϕ_1 only. By applying the read pulses to the near end during ϕ_1, these pulses stretch into ϕ_2 for the bits at the far end of the word-line.

When a static adder is used in the data-path, it is possible to mitigate the effect of the above RC delay. By placing the least-significant bits of the data-path at the end of the word-lines near the drivers, the adder operation (carry-propagation) can start as soon as these bits are read, without waiting for the most-significant bits from the far end. RISC II, however, uses a dynamic ALU circuit with a precharged carry-chain. That chain can only be released after *all* input bits have settled.

Decoding the register-addresses must be done before the corresponding access begins, so that the word-lines remain stable once activated. The chosen timing scheme has the advantage of allowing the register-file decoders to operate during the phases when the word-line drivers are disabled, that is during ϕ_2 and ϕ_4. Thus, no pipeline latches are required at their output, and the congestion in that area is alleviated.

Figure 4.2.2 shows the RISC II timing graph, adapted to the four clock phases and to the data-path of figure 4.1.1. Register reads occur during ϕ_1 and part of ϕ_2; thus, the ALU-operation timing was defined to use the end of ϕ_2 for set-up, and ϕ_3 and part of ϕ_4 for carry propagation. Memory accesses start after the ALU operation has been completed. The effective-address is sent off the chip late in ϕ_4 and during the next ϕ_1. Data or instructions come back into the CPU late in ϕ_3, just in time for the instruction and source-register-numbers to be decoded during ϕ_4. For *write* memory-accesses, data are sent to memory during

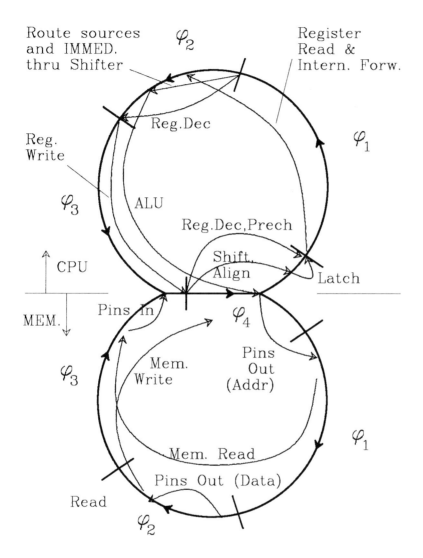

Figure 4.2.2: The RISC II 4-Phase Timing.

ϕ_2 , following the address. This relatively late transfer of the write-data is not a limiting factor for memory chips, because address decoding must occur before the data are needed.

The choice of using the shifter twice per cycle, for operations with diverse timing (sect. 4.1.3), had important implications. The shifter is used for shifts/alignments and for bringing the immediates into the data-path. The fact that it has to be precharged before each use is another reason why four phases per cycle are necessary.

An immediate constant must be routed through the shifter during ϕ_2 . It cannot be routed during ϕ_1 , because the previous instruction may have been a *load* that used the shifter during ϕ_4 for aligning its data. The routing of the immediate constant through the shifter may totally overlap the stretched register read operation during ϕ_2 . In this case, no extra delays are introduced because of this routing. This was our original estimate and an additional reason why it was decided not to spend silicon area for an extra vertical bus for immediates (sect. 4.1.3). However, this balance of delays of the two operations is strongly dependent on the implementation. The routing of immediates may easily extend beyond the read operation. This would introduce extra delays and routing of the immediates would become the critical path leading to the ALU.

4.2.3 The RISC II Timing, Reconsidered after Lay-out

After laying out the chip, its performance was studied with circuit simulation and analysis, based on the actual sizes and resulting parasitic capacitances of the circuit elements. The critical portions of the data-path were simulated with SPICE2 [NaPe73], using the "worst-case-speed" parameters shown in Table 4.2.1. The delays through the rest of the chip were estimated using the timing verifier Crystal [Oust83], which utilizes a simple RC model. Figure 4.2.3 shows some results of that study. Two major deviations from the delay values originally expected made the actual timing noticeably different from the ideal picture of Figure 4.2.1.

The actual length and capacitance of the word-lines is less than originally anticipated. An accurate simulation showed that the "stretching" of the register-read operation into ϕ_2 was small. This puts the routing of the immediate-field into the critical path (§ 4.2.2).

Table 4.2.1: SPICE Parameters (worst-case-speed).						
λ	2.0	μm	**Capacitances:**			
Transistors:			metal	0.14	fF/λ^2	
V_{ET0}	0.9	V	diffusion bulk	0.3	fF/λ^2	
V_{DT0}	-3.2	V	diffusion side-wall	0.3	fF/λ	
V_{DD}	5.0	V	poly over field	0.2	fF/λ^2	
V_{BB}	-2.0	V	gate	1.6	fF/λ^2	
γ	0.75	$V^{1/2}$	gate-src overlap	0.5	fF/λ	
k'	20.7	$\mu A/V^2$	**Resistances:**			
μ_0	600	cm^2/Vs	polysilicon	50	Ω/squ.	
min. electr. channel L	4.0	μm	diffusion	10	Ω/squ.	

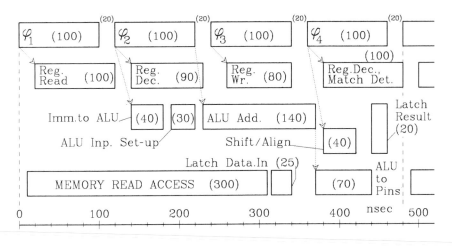

Figure 4.2.3: The RISC II Timing as Simulated after Layout.

Phases 2 and 4 have to be longer than 60ns because register-file decoding is slower than expected. RISC II has 138 registers requiring 276 decoding gates in its two-port overlapping-window register file. Minimizing the size and power dissipation of these gates was crucial because of their large number, even though it led to slower operation. This effect compounds to the delay in the decoding circuits due to the overlapping-window scheme (figure 3.2.1(a)). The decoding gates for the non-overlap registers are 6-input NOR gates with a delay of about 30ns. (Their low-power pull-up has W/L = 0.5, while it is pulling-up $\approx$ 0.25pF of load capacitance, consisting of $45\lambda^2$ of gate capacitance, $200\lambda^2$ of drain-diffusion capacitance, and a 160λ-long polysilicon wire.) However, the overlap registers require OR-AND-INVERT decoding gates, which have a delay of about 70ns. If the circuit of figure 3.2.1(b) had been devised earlier, decoding time for the overlap registers in RISC II could have been reduced to about 40 to 45ns.

Another issue studied is the delay resulting from routing data from the register-file across the shifter to the ALU. Driving busses D and R from busses A and B takes approximately 20ns. The use of busses D and R to feed the ALU -- instead of extending A and B all the way to the latter -- was chosen because it leads to a much less congested layout in the area of SRC, and because it simplifies ALU input multiplexing (sect. 4.1.3). Extending busses A and B all the way to the ALU would have increased their capacitance and slowed down register-reads by about 15ns.

4.2.4 Lessons Learned

Here we present some insights gained during the design of the data-path. They result from comparing the ideal RISC II timing (§ 4.2.1) with the originally planned real timing (§ 4.2.2) and with the actual timing that finally resulted (§ 4.2.3). It has become clear that loss in performance can be attributed to two main reasons:

- Not enough hardware resources were allocated to frequent operations.
- Too many hardware resources were allocated to infrequent operations.

This is yet another expression of the RISC concept: Capabilities added to a circuit in order to speed up some operation(s) will slow down other operations. Thus, the only capabilities that should be added to a circuit are the ones that speed up the most frequently used operations.

The fine balance of the delays on the word-lines and of routing the immediate through the shifter, that was originally sought, was not achieved. The area saved by passing the immediates through the shifter incurred significant performance penalties. By spending extra hardware, we could have eliminated the need for ϕ_2, and thus significantly speed up the RISC II CPU. The extra hardware is not trivial, but would have been worth spending:

- An extra 19-bit vertical bus would be needed on the left side of the ALU for introducing the immediate constants into the data-path.
- A more complicated register-address decoder would be needed to overlap the write-address decoding with the read operation.
- Pull-down transistors would be needed at the far end of the register word-lines to suppress the read-pulses at the end of the read operation and before the beginning of the write operation.

In general, enough specialized resources should be dedicated to the key CPU operations.

On the other hand, the area occupied by the cross-bar shifter and by its associated input latch/driver, SRC, is significant, and so is the bus congestion caused by its busses R and L in the $DST-SRC$ area. This introduces delays into the frequently used path between ALU and the register-file, as discussed at the end of the last subsection. The shifter could have been placed on the right-hand side of the ALU, and immediates introduced into the data-path through a separate bus. It would still consume precious space in the overloaded, critical horizontal length of the data-path, but the data transfer delays would be reduced. In most programs, shifting by an arbitrary amount occurs rarely (chapter 2). Shifting by one or two bits, as required for multiplications and for conversions of array indexes to byte addresses, could be performed in the ALU. Our conclusion is that an arbitrary-amount shifter does not belong in the critical part of the data-path; it could be included somewhere else, accessible only by slower-executing instructions. For example, it could be placed near $DIMM$ (fig. 4.1.1) where it would also be useful in aligning data from memory.

4.3   The RISC II Control

The main consequence of a reduced instruction set is the dramatic reduction of
the silicon resources required for control. The RISC II opcode-decoder:

*   occupies only 0.5 % of the chip area,
*   has 0.7 % of the transistors,
*   required less than 2 % of our total design and layout time.

This opcode-decoder is the equivalent of the micro-program memory in microcoded CPU's. The RISC II control section occupies only 10 % of the chip area.
These figures stand in sharp contrast to the usual size of control in contemporary
microprocessors [Fitz81] [Beye81]:

*   the M68000 control section is 68% of the chip area;
*   the Z8000 control section is 53% of the chip area;
*   the iAPX-432-01 control section is 65% of the chip area;
*   the HP "Focus" 32-bit CPU has 78% of its transistors in its microcode
    ROM.

Although the organization of the RISC II control could be considered as
"random logic", it only required half a person-year of design and layout effort.

4.3.1 Organization of the RISC II Control

Figure 4.3.1 shows the organization of the RISC II control. Registers are tagged
with a number (1), (2), or (3) to indicate the pipeline stage to which the information they hold belongs. Thus, the registers marked "(1)" hold the information of
the instruction being currently fetched, while those marked "(2)" hold information relating to the currently executing instruction. This latter information will
flow into the "(3)-registers" during the next cycle, if necessary. This flow of
information among the pipeline registers freezes when the pipeline is suspended
for a data-memory-access.

Decoding the incoming instruction is particularly easy in RISC II, because of the simple instruction format with fields of fixed size and position (sect. 3.1.4). RISC II does not have a single physically-integrated instruction register. Instead, it has multiple instruction-field registers, each one close to the place where it is needed.

- Some instruction fields may have multiple interpretations, depending on the instruction. They pose no problem: copies of the same field are latched at *all* places of possible use, and the unnecessary ones are thrown away later on. Examples:
  → Fields <18:14>, <13>, and <4:0> may be parts of an immediate constant, or they may be R_{s1} , *IMMflag*, and R_{s2} respectively.
  → Field <22:19> may be part of R_d , or it may be the jump-condition.
- One instruction field, that must be used as soon as the instruction arrives into the CPU, may originate from two different places in the instruction, depending on the opcode:
  → The second register to be read via *busB* is R_{s2} (<4:0>) for most instructions, but it is R_d (<23:19>) for *store* instructions.
  This does pose a problem. The selection of the appropriate origin may not wait until the opcode has been decoded through the normal decoder. Instead, a special fast gate is used to distinguish *store* from *non−store* instructions. The particular choice of opcodes allows this distinction to be made very quickly, based on whether instr<30:29>=11.

The register-numbers and the immediate-constant move through the pipeline of instruction-field-registers and are used at the appropriate place and time. Figure 4.3.1 shows their organization and should be compared with figure 4.1.1. The *imm*-field-register-(2) is *DIMM* in fig. 4.1.1. The register-number field-registers-(1) are not shown in fig. 4.1.1, for simplicity. Figure 4.3.1 also shows the circuit which detects data-dependencies and initiates internal-forwarding; R_{s1} and R_{s2} of pipeline-stage-(1) are compared with R_d of pipeline-stage-(2) for equality.

The 7-bit op-code, together with one bit of state information, is decoded to generate 30 bits of decoded-opcode information. Op-codes are decoded *once per*

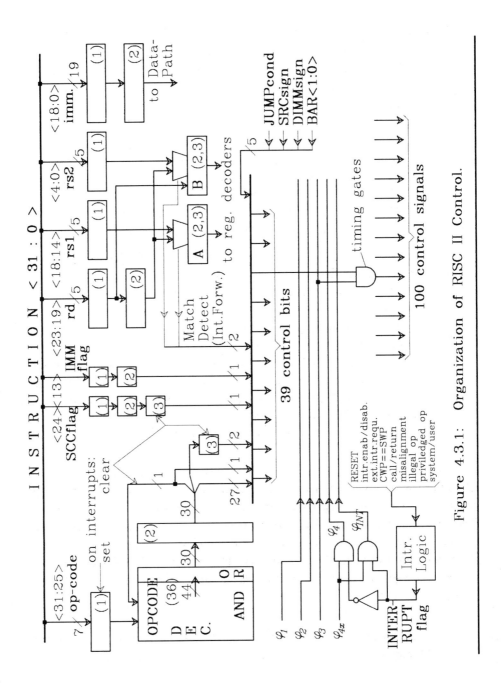

Figure 4.3.1:   Organization of RISC II Control.

cycle, and the one bit of state serves to distinguish between a normal cycle and a memory-data-access cycle during which the rest of the pipeline activity is suspended.

Twenty-eight of the 30 decoded-opcode bits are used during the second (computation) stage of the pipeline. Two others, together with *SCCflag* (set-condition-codes flag), are used to control the activities during the last stage of the pipeline, which is the only one that modifies the user-visible state of the CPU. These three bits control writing into R_d, *PSW*, or the *CCs*. On interrupts, they get cleared, thus effectively aborting the instruction that was executing †. Also, on interrupts, the op-code latch gets loaded with a special hardwired instruction, *calli*. This instruction calls the interrupt handler, changes the current window (sect. 3.2.2), and saves *LSTPC* into R_{25} of the new (free) window. In this way, the interrupted instruction can be restarted. More information on interrupts can be found in Appendix A.

Besides the 30 decoded-opcode bits, nine more bits of information are involved in the generation of the control signals. They are (see fig. 4.3.1):

- **SCCflag:** set-condition-codes flag from the instruction.
- **IMMflag:** immediate flag from the instruction, specifying whether **short-SOURCE2** is R_{s2} or an immediate (fig. 3.1.2).
- **Match-Detect:** detection of data-dependencies among second and third pipeline stages, and initiation of internal-forwarding (§ 3.3.1).
- **JUMPcond:** the result of evaluating the condition for a conditional jump.
- **SRCsign:** the sign-bit of the *SRC* latch, used to control sign-extension during *shift* instructions.
- **DIMMsign:** the sign-bit of the *DIMM* latch, used to control sign-extension of immediate operands, or during *load* instructions.

---

† An interrupt that occurs during the memory-cycle of a *store* instruction will *not* prevent the memory-write from occurring, if it may occur (i.e. if a page-fault was not the interrupt cause). The same *store* instruction will be re-executed when the interrupt-handler returns, re-writing exactly the same data into exactly the same memory location. Notice that the interrupt cause may *not* have been an address-misalignment, since misalignment-interrupts only occur during the address-calculation cycle.

- **BAR:** the Byte-Address-Register, used in detecting address misalignments.

The control signals are generated by ANDing one or more of the above 39 bits with one or more of the clock phases (as in polyphase microcoded implementations). RISC II uses four clock phases, as discussed in sect. 4.2.2. These are externally supplied but the fourth one of them, ϕ_{4x} , is internally "split" into two mutually exclusive phases, ϕ_4 and ϕ_{INT} . Normally, ϕ_4 is issued; however, when an interrupt occurs, ϕ_{INT} replaces it and sets and clears all the crucial bits, as discussed above.

There are 100 control signals, half of them for the data-path, and half of them for the control section. These include multiple copies for local uses, clock phases with no control qualification, and decoded-opcode bits with no clock qualification. Most of the 100 timing gates which generate them are very simple:
- 87 timing gates have not more than one clock input;
- 70 timing gates have not more than one clock input and not more than one control-bit input.

Only 18 of the control signals depend on control bits other than the decoded-opcode bits.

Thus, the organization of the RISC II control is simple and straightforward. There is a finite-state-machine with 7 inputs, 30 outputs, and only 2 states. Its outputs are combined with 4 clock phases to generate the control signals. Because not all timing gates are simple 2-input AND gates, and because some control bits are generated outside the FSM, one may find elements of "random logic" organization in the RISC II control. However, that is not the issue. The issue is that that control section has a straightforward organization, that it is easy to understand, and that it required only six person-months of design *and* layout effort.

4.3.2 Simplicity of the RISC II Control

In RISC II, a few dozen bits of information are enough to control the execution of an instruction. This number stands in sharp contrast to the much larger number of microprogram bits required to execute each instruction in typical microprogrammed machines. We attribute this reduction of required information to the uniformity of the execution of the RISC instructions. All RISC instructions follow the pattern: *read-sources, operate, appropriately-route-the-result,* and they follow it with the same fixed timing. Thus, the only information which the instruction-decoder needs to generate is whether or not a certain control signal must be activated during the execution of the current instruction. The particular time during which the control signal might be activated is known in advance and hardwired into the gate that drives it.

An important characteristic of the instruction-decoder is its simplicity as a combinational circuit. It decodes 8 inputs which can be in one of 56 relevant states: 23 single-cycle instructions, 16 two-cycle instructions, or illegal (unassigned) op-codes. It has 36 distinct product terms and 30 outputs. The average number of product terms participating in the generation of an output is 1.47. Thus, if it were to be implemented using a general PLA, the OR plane would be very sparse: 36×30 crosspoints containing only 44 transistors. For that reason, we used a generalized decoder with a single row of OR gates, instead. This implementation consumes about 60 % less area than the PLA implementation, and it is significantly faster.

We attribute the low number of product terms per decoded-instruction bit to the fact that the instruction set is highly orthogonal, and that orthogonality maps into the op-codes and into the data-path. The low density of assigned opcodes, using only 39 legal opcodes out of 64 (see Appendix A), also had a positive effect. Consider the following examples (x's mean "don't care"):

Class of opcodes:	Instructions:	Hardware function controled:
01xxxxx	load/store	two-cycle instruction: set state-bit to *pipeline-suspension-cycle*
01xxxx1	PC-relative load/store	place *PC* onto *busD* on ϕ_2 ; don NOT place *busA* onto *busD* on ϕ_2
0001x01	PC-relative jump/call	
0101x1x	signed load	sign-extender/zero-filler
00011xx	conditional control transf. (jmp/ret)	together with JUMPcond, determines whether to place *INC* or the ALU output onto *busOUT* on ϕ_4

Each one of these classes of instructions is decoded using a single product term. The selection of the 39 opcodes within a 2^6 opcode space was done with the purpose of minimizing the size of the decoder; it required only a 2 person-hours effort. The selection of the AND and OR terms of the decoder was done in 2 further person-hours. These numbers demonstrate the simplicity of the RISC II control.

One may consider a circuit with such a small and simple control section as a "hardware engine" rather than a High-Level-Language Computer. However, as section 3.4 has shown, this circuit executes compiled High-Level-Language programs faster than several popular commercial processors. Its compiler and optimizer were easily written, and the machine code is no more than 50 % larger than that of other processors.

4.4   Design Metrics of RISC II

Table 4.4.1 presents several design metrics for RISC II. It gives the total absolute values for the chip area, number of transistors, power consumption, number of rectangles, and approximate design and layout time, as well as the percentages of these values attributed to various CPU sub-functions.

The register-number decoders and shift-amount decoder were included in the data-path. The control section is subdivided into opcode-decoder, instruction-and-control-registers, and timing-gates (see Figure 4.3.1), as well as other specialized circuits (condition codes, jump condition, interrupt logic, window numbers) and wiring. Areas are separately given for the power wiring (ground and +5V) in the data-path and control sections. For the rest of the metrics, the power wiring of the data-path and of the control is included in their various sub-blocks, from which it was difficult to separate.

The numbers given for power dissipation use worst-case-power parameters, which are different from those shown in table 3.1: $V_{TE0} = 0.7V$, $V_{DT0} = -3.8V$, *lateral-diffusion* $= 0.7\mu m$, $k' = 30.7 \,\mu A/V^2$.

The layout tool used was *Caesar* [Oust81], which allows only rectangles with horizontal and vertical edges. We are convinced that the area penalty paid for this restriction was minimal †, and that it was well worth the resulting simplifications in the layout task and in our CAD tools. The number of "drawn rectangles" counts the rectangles explicitly specified in the *Caesar* data base. This number exaggerates the number of rectangles actually placed by the designer. It counts a slightly modified copy of a cell as a totally different cell, as is the case with most timing-gates. The number of "instantiated rectangles" counts all geometry after arrays and calls have been expanded.

Design and layout times are approximate. The totals for data-path and control are higher than the sum of the parts, because they include some general, organizational work. The elapsed time was half a year (times one person) for the micro-architecture design, plus two years (times two persons) for everything else.

---

† The register-cell is limited by fundamental line widths in both directions, and could not be smaller with inclined lines. The shifter's width could be reduced by 16 λ (= 0.3 % of the chip width) using 45° lines [SKPS82].

Table 4.4.1: RISC II Design Metrics.

Part	% Area	% Transistors	% Power (worst case)	Rectangles % Drawn	Rectangles % Inst.	Regularity	~% Time Design	~% Time Layout
Data-Path: (tot.)	**50.**	**92.6**	**57.**	**23.5**	**90.0**	**74.**	**13.**	**10.**
Register File	33.3	73.4	39.3	2.2	70.0	624	3.3	2.3
(storage array)	(27.5)	(64.6)	(34.8)	(0.3)	(60.1)	(3640)		
(decoders)	(5.8)	(8.8)	(4.5)	(1.9)	(9.9)	(104)		
ALU	2.7	5.1	4.0	4.1	4.5	21	2.1	1.1
Shifter	4.3	4.8	2.9	5.3	6.4	24	1.0	1.5
(cross-bar array)	(2.8)	(2.5)	(.0)	(0.1)	(3.4)	(480)	(.5)	(.5)
(inp.latch/dr, decoder)	(1.5)	(2.3)	(2.9)	(5.2)	(3.0)	(11)	(.5)	(1.0)
PC's	2.8	5.6	4.2	3.8	4.7	24	1.3	1.1
Other MUX/latch/drivers	3.2	3.7	6.6	8.1	4.4	11	2.8	3.3
Power wiring	3.9							
Control: (tot.)	**10.**	**5.7**	**13.**	**54.4**	**5.8**	**2.1**	**7.**	**10.**
Opcode Decoder	.5	.7	1.0	2.0	1.6	7.2	1.1	.6
Instr.&Control Registers	1.6	1.9	4.7	5.5	1.6	5.7	.5	.2
CC's, Jmp Cond, Interr.	.8	1.3	2.4	10.5	1.2	2.1	1.3	1.2
Window Number	.5	.5	1.0	4.9	.5	1.8	.5	.4
Timing Gates/Drivers	1.0	1.3	3.9	18.5	1.0	1.1	1.7	1.8
Wiring (non-power)	4.8			13.0	.7	1.0		4.3
Power wiring	.9							
Periphery: (tot.)	**40.**	**1.7**	**30.**	**22.1**	**4.2**	**3.5**	**2.4**	**3.6**
Bonding Pads	10.3	1.7	30.0	3.1	2.7	16.6	.8	1.5
Wiring (non-power)	13.0			9.5		1.5	.8	1.7
Power wiring	9.2			1.5	.1	1.0	.8	.4
Unused area (logo's)	7.2			8.0	.6	1.4		
Micro-Archit. Design							9.	
Debugging/Verification							2.	
Document. & Overhead							27.	16.
Total CPU %	100.0	100.0	100.0	100.0	100.0		60.	40.
Total CPU Abs. Value	14.9 $M\Lambda^2$	40.76 K	1.9 Watts	23.5 K	460. K	19.6	5250 man-hours	

The total of 5250 man-hours given corresponds to 2.7 man-years, and is lower than the real elapsed time because of other activities occurring in parallel (courses, other research). It does not include work performed after the chip was submitted for fabrication (i.e. more documentation and testing).

In section 4.3 the size of the RISC II control section was compared to that of other micro-processors. Here, we compare the number of transistors, the regularity, and the design and layout effort for the whole chip (data from [Fitz81]):

CPU:	Transistors K	Regularity -	Design person-months	Layout person-months
RISC I	44	22	15	12
RISC II	41	20	18	12
M68000	68	12	100	70
Z8000	18	5	60	70
iAPX-432-01	110	8	170	90

When these numbers are combined with the performance comparisons of sect. 3.4.3, the advantages of the Reduced Instruction Set approach become evident.

Chapter 5

Debugging and Testing RISC II

This chapter describes the method used and the experience gained in the process of debugging the RISC II logic design and layout and in the functional testing of the RISC II chips. The fact that RISC II chips worked correctly on first silicon is a result of both the simple architecture and the effectiveness of the CAD environment that was used. The fact that RISC II chips were easily tested, without the need to use the scan-in/scan-out loops, is again due to the simple architecture with a readily accessible CPU state.

In this chapter we deal only with logic debugging and functional testing. Timing analysis of the critical data-path and control circuits was done with *SPICE2* [NaPe73]. To check that the timing constraints were met, the timing verifier *Crystal* [Oust83] was used after the whole chip was laid-out. Geometrical layout rules were checked with *Lyra* [ArOu82]. For further discussions on circuit simulation and timing see Sherburne's thesis [Sher84].

5.1   Logic Debugging Tools and Methods

The sophisticated simulation tools available in today's CAD environments make it feasible to debug a VLSI design almost completely *before* fabrication. Such debugging is desirable for several reasons.

Software simulation has a faster turn-around time and lower cost than prototype fabrication, and this is likely to stay true in the next years. Even if this situation should be reversed some day, due to major advances in the implementation of IC chips, software simulation can typically not be avoided. If a prototype returned from fabrication does not perform as expected when plugged into the system or test set-up, how can one find out why it might not work properly? Unless some revolutionary new method of hardware testing is discovered, our capability to monitor or modify the value of internal nodes in a VLSI chip is very limited. Mechanical probing is heavily constrained in terms of number and size of nodes, and because of the capacitive loading introduced into the circuit. Scanning electron microscope methods cannot simultaneously monitor many fast-changing nodes. Software simulation, on the contrary, offers the capability of monitoring and changing the values of internal nodes. This is crucial in complex VLSI systems with limited controlability/observability. Simulation is thus often the only way to gain understanding of the causes of malfunctioning circuits.

Hierarchical design and multi-level simulation tools make it possible to debug a VLSI design at a level of abstraction which is higher than transistors and capacitors. This makes possible a properly structured design employing early debugging, before bad assumptions or errors lead to poor design decisions. For complicated systems, this hierarchical approach also makes the task of debugging manageable by checking each block at the proper level of abstraction.

The RISC II design was done at four levels:

- architecture (ISP),
- micro-architecture (RTL),
- gates (logic), and
- layout (circuit & mask geometry).

The architecture level corresponds to the system specification. The RISC I & II architecture was described using the *ISPS* notation [Corc80] [BaMa78]. The corresponding simulator was used to test the architecture, but it was too slow to run large programs. A "special purpose" RISC simulator program was written [Tami81] and was used in conjunction with the RISC compiler and assembler for evaluating the RISC performance.

The micro-architecture level corresponds to a register-transfer description, roughly like the one given in chapter 4. The *Slang* language and simulator [VDFo82] were used for this level, as described below in § 5.1.1.

At the gate level, we only used diagrams on paper. Because that level is quite close to the final layout, the lack of machine-readable description was not important.

At the layout level, *Esim* [TermES] was used for switch-level simulation of the circuit that was extracted from the layout, as described below in § 5.1.2 and § 5.1.3.

5.1.1 SLANG: Simulation and Debugging at the RTL Level

Slang is a LISP-based hardware description language and event-driven-simulator [VDFo82] that is suitable for describing and simulating digital systems at mixed levels of abstraction. We did use it in such a mixed-mode description and simulation:

- *Gate-level:* Some parts, such as the timing-gates in the control section, were described at the gate-level.
- *Gate-Vector-level:* Some latches in the data-path, whose proper internal operation needed verification, were described as two cross-coupled 32-bit vectors. Bitwise boolean operations on 32-bit integers were used for that purpose.
- *Register-level:* Other latches were described at the register-level, by using assignment operations on 32-bit integers.
- *Block-level:* Parts of the system were described as a block, using a LISP program. Such was the case for the off-chip memory, the register-file and shifter plus their decoders, the opcode decoder, the interrupt logic, and the jump-condition PLA.

- *Real-Polarity-level:* The data-path busses were described using their real polarities. This was done in order to verify the correctness of the design, since some of them are used with different polarities at different times.

- *Symbolic-Polarity-level:* For other values, no actual polarity was specified; they were just simulated as *ON* or *OFF*.

- *Symbolic-Value-level:* Some of the node-values were symbolic constants or lists of objects. Such was the case for opcodes and instructions, which were both described at the assembly level. This mnemonic representation was very helpful. It was easy to implement because of the LISP environment.

Difficulties were encountered in describing and simulating bi-directional pass-transistors, like the ones in the register-cell and in the shifter. To solve this problem, *Slang* was modified to permit multiple sources driving the same node, provided that one of them is characterized as "stronger" than the others. Then, the bi-directional transistors were modeled as two simultaneous connections in opposite directions, with each one transmitting a value in its own direction. This has the undesirable side-effect of creating a feedback loop in the simulated circuit, which is not present in the real circuit. In our case, the storage effect that the feedback loop gives did not bother us, because the corresponding real busses do exhibit dynamic capacitive storage, and because external sources, which are "stronger" than the pass-transistors, can break the loop. However, this fictitious loop effect may be a real problem when this same simulation technique is applied to other systems.

Slang allows nodes to have an *"unknown"* value and uses this value during initialization and when conflicts of multiple sources arise. The technique was very useful in making sure that the RISC II chip can be initialized using the external pins alone. A minor problem had to be overcome in a few cases. When only some of the bits of a word are unknown, *Slang* will assign the value *unknown* to the whole word. These words thus had to be split into multiple parts, and the corresponding hardware into multiple nodes, leading to a more cumbersome description.

Slang should normally be used during the micro-architecture design, before layout work begins. In our case, however, it was used only after the data-path was laid-out. No errors in the data-path design were found, owing probably to the processor's simplicity. On the other hand, 5 to 10 design errors were uncovered in the control section and were corrected before layout began. Simulation for debugging was done using multiple small test-programs as input. The correctness of the design was checked by manually looking at the simulation results. This manual checking was not very time-consuming, and thus no need was felt to use the architecture simulator for automatic result checking. The set of test programs was believed to be fairly complete. Nevertheless, later during the switch-level simulation a design error was found that was not covered by the test-programs (an instruction setting the carry-bit, immediately followed by an instruction using the carry-bit). This shows that our ad-hoc approach to test generation is not satisfactory.

5.1.2 Node Naming and Circuit Extraction

Throughout the layout, a conscious effort was made to flag as many of the nodes in every cell as possible with names. This practice turned out to be very useful for documentation and for debugging. About half a dozen layout errors were uncovered early in the debugging phase merely through the analysis of the node-naming error diagnostics of the circuit extraction program. The preferred names were the ones used for the corresponding nodes in the *Slang* description. Good and consistent naming conventions proved to be important but were not easy to devise in the early stages of the design. Polarity information was included in as many of the names as possible.

We used *Mextra* [FitzME] to extract the transistor and interconnection list from the layout. The program issues two types of diagnostic messages:

(1) reports of the discovery of two different names on the same electric node, and

(2) reports of the same name appearing on more than one node.

Some of those messages correspond to legal situations. Situation (1) may arise when a node has multiple functions, and (2) may result from cells that are replicated many times for different bits or functional units. Other messages correspond to layout errors. Type-(1) messages indicate accidental short-circuits or erroneous wiring of output A to input B and of output B to input A. Type-(2)

messages indicate missing connections if there are more node instances with a certain name than there should normally be according to the design. *Mextra* follows a certain naming convention that allows it to separate type-(1) messages into legal and erroneous cases, and to report them separately. However, no similar mechanism is available for messages of the latter type.

5.1.3 Co-Simulation at the RTL and Extracted-Switch Levels

The transistor and interconnection list that was extracted from the layout, was simulated with the switch-level simulator *Esim* [TermES]. A number of unconventional circuits had to be looked at carefully, to decide whether their simulation would present any problems. If necessary, the circuit-description file was hand-patched to overcome such problems:

- The shifter presented no problem, because *Esim* knows how to handle bi-directional transistors.
- The register cell itself, presented no problem, but its interface to the busses did. Firstly *Esim* would not detect the cell-disturbance that could occur if a read-operation were attempted via a non-precharged bus; the reason is that *Esim* believes that a static pull-up is always stronger than a capacitive load. Secondly, *Esim* could not handle internal forwarding correctly, because in the real chip that depends on the *DST* driver being stronger than the register cell; *Esim*, on the other hand, always assumes that a pull-down is stronger than a pull-up.
- The bootstrap-drivers for the register word-lines could be simulated correctly, with the only exception that an *unknown* decoder output would cause the *unknown* value on its word-line to propagate onto the bootstrapping clock. The reason is again the lack of understanding that a strong pull-up is present.
- Some static latches in the control section have a long depletion transistor which is used as a feedback resistor. *Esim* considers all depletion transistors with gate and source tied together as pull-ups (!), and thus fails to simulate those latches correctly.

A simulator that understands that some transistors are stronger than others would solve the above problems, provided that it also handles depletion transistors correctly.

Debugging a system at the switch level is very difficult, because of the large number of nodes that have to be watched, and because the correct values that these nodes should have are not always obvious. For that reason, *Slang* has been written in such a way that it can execute together with *Esim*. Two lists of "corresponding nodes" are defined by the designer. *Slang* will drive the *Esim* nodes on the first list with the values that their corresponding nodes have in *Slang*, then perform a simulation step at both levels, and then compare the values that the "corresponding nodes" of the second list have in *Slang* and in *Esim*, and print any discrepancies. In this way, the results of the switch-level simulation are automatically checked against the debugged RTL description. During RISC II debugging, the values of 1300 circuit nodes (single bits) were being compared for equality after each clock phase transition. Besides the ease provided by the automatic checking, the method is also very helpful in identifying the cause of a discrepancy and finding the offending layout error. When checking is done automatically, the values of many nodes throughout the chip can be checked, and thus, the first discrepancy reported is usually very close to its cause.

The switch-level simulation uncovered 11 mistakes:

- one timing design error on a scan-in/scan-out loop (this was not uncovered by *Slang*, because *Slang* does not know about these loops);
- one missing flip-flop design error (this is the one mentioned at the end of § 5.1.1, that the *Slang* test programs weren't testing for);
- one flip-flop not being cleared on ϕ_I, as it should;
- an error in the programming of a decoder;
- one connection to the wrong point;
- one case of reversed connections; and
- five cases of connections to the wrong polarity.

This shows that most of the errors were cases of wrong connection. *Mextra*'s name-checking did not catch them either because the node naming was incomplete, or because *Mextra* only looks at the names on electricly connected points and does not check the consistency of input and output signal names on simple gates.

5.2   Testing the RISC II Chips

The RISC II layout was submitted for fabrication to MOSIS at $\lambda=2\mu m$, and to
XEROX PARC at $\lambda=1.5\mu m$. Twenty-eight chips were received back from
MOSIS two months later, and five chips were received from XEROX in one and
a half months. Five out of the 28 MOSIS chips were rejected by visual inspec-
tion, and 3 of the remaining 5 that were bonded and tested were found functionally correct. The fastest one of them run at a 500 nsec cycle-time. One out of
the 5 XEROX chips was found functionally correct, except for some bad bits in a
few registers. It run at a 330 nsec cycle-time.

All the digital IC's designed in our group at U.C.Berkeley during the last
three years have been debugged by simulation of the extracted layout. Our
experience has invariably been that chips carefully debugged in this way are
functionally correct on first silicon. This was true for all of the following big
projects:

- RISC I,
- FFT cordic rotator (Lioupis, Wold),
- RISC II,
- RISC Instruction Cache

It demonstrates the viability and the effectiveness of this debugging method.

The present section deals with the functional testing of the RISC II CPU
chips. It describes the hardware set-up and the testing strategy that was used,
and it discusses the usefulness of scan-in/scan-out loops.

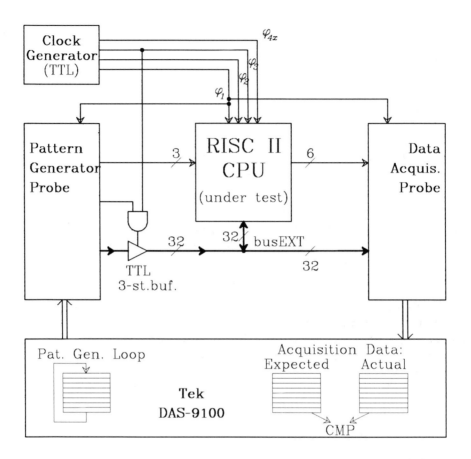

Figure 5.2.1:   RISC II Testing Set-Up.

5.2.1 Testing Set-up and Strategy

Figure 5.2.1 shows the set-up that was used for testing the RISC II CPU chips. A Digital Analyzer (Tek DAS-9100) was used for pattern generation (PG), for data acquisition, and for comparing the acquired to the expected values. We preferred the use of an external clock generator, rather than synthesizing the clock phases with the pattern generator. It reduces the number of different patterns that need to be generated, since the chip itself only needs a new pattern every 4 phases. The external clock generator also allows short non-overlap periods and individually-variable clock phases. External tri-state buffers were required, because the particular DAS that was used offered no tri-state PG channels.

Testing is done by having the chip execute normal instructions, which are supplied by the PG. Data for *load* instructions are also supplied by the PG. The address stream produced by the CPU chip is recorded, and compared to the expected one. Data originating from *store* instructions can also be recorded, by using ϕ_2 as the acquisition clock.

Because of the simple architecture, the small CPU state, and the single-cycle execution of instructions, the RISC II CPU chip has very good controlability and observability. Regardless of its previous state, the chip can be initialized to a useful state in only 3 cycles:

- hold the *RESET* pin high for one cycle ($NXTPC \leftarrow 80000000_H$);
- *putpsw*: $PSW \leftarrow R_0 + imm$ (initialize CWP, SWP, interrupts);
- *add*: $R_d \leftarrow R_0 + imm$ (initialize register R_d).

Of course, it would take about 150 cycles to initialize all 138 registers, but one only needs to do that when testing for defects in the register-file. Once a few registers have been loaded, instructions can be tested, and the result of any instruction can be read from the pins in one cycle:

- *jump-indexed always to* $R_d + R_0$,

where R_d is the destination register of the instruction to be tested. (*Getpsw*, *getlpc*, and PC-relative instructions can be used to read the *PSW* or the *PC*'s). Except for the *PSW*, the *PC*'s, and the registers, all other storage devices in the CPU are initialized and used within the execution cycle of any instruction that uses them. Thus, they are directly controlable and observable by that instruction.

The test programs used were similar or identical to those used during debugging with *Slang* (§ 5.1.1). The same comments apply here. The tests performed are believed to be fairly complete, but there is no proof of that. Our ad-hoc approach to the problem of test generation is simply due to the lack of a good theory and suitable CAD tools.

5.2.2 Scan-In/Scan-Out Loops

Scan-in/scan-out (SISO) capability [WiAn73] [EiWi77] [FrSp81] is added to chips in order to increase the controlability and observability of their internal state from the pins. It can be implemented by organizing all latches as shift-registers and by providing serial ports for reading and writing into them. In the RISC II CPU, three latches, situated at central positions, have SISO capability: *DST*, *SRC*, and the latch holding the output of the opcode-decoder. The two former ones form a single 64-bit loop, while the latter one forms a 32-bit loop by itself. Each of these two loops uses separate dedicated pads and wires for their shift-clock and serial-I/O. In this way, if the normal connections of the CPU with the external world are defective, the loops may still provide access to the chip's interior.

The cost of the SISO loops in the RISC II CPU is not high: Area-wise, they consume only about 1% of the data-path, about 3% of the control section, and 10% of the pads. Speed-wise, they slow the machine cycle down by about 1%. However, the cost of using the loops for testing the chip is high. First, to load values into them, or to read their contents, 32 or 64 cycles are required, as opposed to the 1 to 4 cycles required for accessing the same latches with normal instructions (§ 5.2.1). Second, reading/writing via the loops requires that the normal CPU clocks be stopped and that the SISO-shift clocks be activated. Third, the whole mode of operation of the SISO loops is much different from the rest of the chip, thus requiring significant human effort and additional software tools for their use.

There are several situations in which chips can be put in a test set-up:

(1) for debugging a design;
(2) for debugging a fabrication process, and finding out what particular circuit is not working in a series of defective dies; or
(3) for identifying operational dies for packaging and use.

In our view, number (1) above should be used only to *verify* that the design is correct; debugging should be done in software, as discussed earlier in this chapter. Number (2) above can be done with dies specifically designed for that purpose; it does not need to be done with production chips. Thus, we believe that the usefulness of SISO loops should only be considered in the context of product testing, i.e. purpose (3) above. SISO loops can always increase the controlability and observability (C/O) of those dies where a certain type of defects would have disconnected the SISO latches from the external world without the presence of the serial path. However, for correctly designed and defect-less dies, an increase in testability is not always present. In our view, SISO loops should be evaluated according to how much they increase the C/O of *operational* chips.

In RISC II, the data-path SISO loop offers no increase in C/O in a correctly working chip, because normal instructions can also be used to copy values between registers and *DST* or *SRC*. The control SISO does increase the C/O of the opcode-decoder's output, because normal instructions cannot read that output; neither are there any instructions that can load an arbitrary value into these latches. However, we consider that increase in C/O to be of limited usefulness. The bits in that latch control so many things throughout the CPU, that even if only one of them is incorrect, chances are that most instructions will not work at all. From that point of view, the observability of the latch is very high. On the other hand, loading an arbitrary pattern into that latch -- one that does not correspond to any real instruction -- is of very limited usefulness. It is normally very difficult to devise new ways of getting a data-path to perform useful transfers that do not already exist; this is especially true in RISC II, where the timing information is hardwired in the timing gates.

For all the above reasons, the SISO loops in the RISC II CPU have *not* been used in testing it, just like it had happened with RISC I [FoVP82]. For these reasons, we consider this style of design-for-testability to have limited usefulness in the case of micro-architectures with readily accessible internal state. For bus-oriented chips, with reduced C/O of their internal state, we suggest that an alternative style of design-for-testability be considered before resorting to SISO loops. When a latch is close to some bus, consider connecting it to that bus for test purposes; this may not be more expensive than adding SISO capability. Such a parallel connection will usually be faster and easier to use than a SISO loop. Of course, if all latches are connected to a single bus, they will all become inaccessible if that bus does not work; but - again - we are only interested in testing for working chips. For chips that are dominated by random logic and that have few or no busses, SISO loops may still be a good solution.

Chapter 6

Additional Hardware Support
for General-Purpose Computations

Chapter 2 studied the nature of general-purpose computations as expressed in von Neumann languages. It was seen that a few simple operations account for most of the execution time and that high performance depends mostly on

- exploitation of fine-grain parallelism,
- fast addressing and operand accessing,
- fast decision making and branching, and
- fast floating-point operations (in numeric applications).

This suggests that it is more effective to use special devices that provide fast access to instructions and operands than to use precious chip area for the implementation of complex instructions.

The Berkeley Reduced-Instruction-Set-Computer experiment, which was presented in chapters 3, 4, and 5, has investigated this direction in computer architecture. RISC I and II provide pipelined execution of simple instructions in an environment where local variables are readily accessible. Section 3.4 gave an evaluation of the experiment, showing both the viability and the advantages of simple instruction sets.

Any hardware resources that remain available after a pipelined data-path and its simple controller have been implemented should be spent as effectively as possible for increasing performance. According to chapter 2, this means providing fast access to the most frequently used operands, fast compare-and-branch operations, and fast number crunching for numeric applications. The first two of these issues are considered in this chapter. The latter one -- number-crunching -- is not considered in this dissertation.

Enhancements intended to providing the above support should be included in a processor according to a "priority list" that depends on the hardware resources (e.g. silicon area) available at a given time. We believe that these priorities are as follows:

1. Register File for frequently used scalar variables,
2. Instruction Cache with support for fast decision making,
3. Data Cache for non-scalar operands.

This ordering results from their relative cost and pay-off. A register file, even of modest size, for scalar variables allows high performance gains. An instruction cache is larger in size but is essential in feeding a fast data-path with new instructions. A data cache has less of a visible effect in an architecture where many of the operands, namely the scalar variables, are already in registers. Separate instruction and data caches are proposed here for two reasons. First, independent memory ports are desirable for parallel instruction-fetching and data-accessing (§ 3.3.2, 3.3.3); second, each one of these two cache types can be structured in a different way to take best advantage of the peculiarities of its usage. Such organizations are proposed below in § 6.3 and § 6.4, after the issue of fast access to scalar variables has been discussed in § 6.1 and § 6.2. Section 6.5 deals with another important issue: moving data into and out of a processor's main memory.

6.1   Multi-Window Register Files versus Cache Memories
for Scalar Variables

Section 3.2 presented the organization of the RISC multi-window register file and explained how it provides fast access to the frequently used local scalar variables. That register file acts as a small and fast buffer for the top of the stack of procedure activation records, that is, for the most recently used local variables. In that respect, a multi-window register file is similar to a cache memory. This section investigates the similarities and the differences between them.

6.1.1   The Various Kinds of Locality of Reference

The locality of the memory references made by a program has usually been studied by statistical methods in a "black box" approach, without looking at the underlying program properties which cause it (see for example [Smit82]). However, a study of the way programs access memory, like the study in chapter 2, shows that this locality has interesting properties arising from the nature of computations. Memory references can be distinguished into three categories, with different locality properties each:

- *Instructions:* Instruction-fetches are read-only accesses. They are sequential in small blocks -- between *if* or *call* or *loop* statements. Locality arises from the repeated accesses to instructions inside loops. Since programs spend most of their time in small inner loops, this locality is high.
- *Scalar Variables:* Scalars occupy a single memory location, and hence, that fixed location is accessed whenever the variable is used. As noted throughout chapter 2, some scalar variables are heavily used during execution. These tend to be few in number, declared locally in their procedure, and used as array-indexes, counters, pointers, flags, or temporary storage locations. For example, in the critical loop of *fgrep* (fig. 2.4.1), out of the 29 operand accesses per iteration, 18 are made to 4 local scalars, 2 are made to 1 global scalar, and 9 are made to non-scalars. These facts show the high locality of the references to the few scalars in critical loops. They are not unrelated to the way the human mind works by hierarchically breaking big tasks into smaller ones, and by only dealing with a few objects/concepts at each level.

- *Non-Scalar Variables:* Arrays and structures occupy many memory locations each, and accesses are *not* made to the same location each time. Usually, certain elements of a few non-scalar variables are accessed once or a few times, and then accesses shift to "neighboring" elements of those variables (chapter 2). "Neighborhood" here, may or may not be actual proximity in virtual address space, depending on the type of the accessed data structure.

Cache memories usually treat all memory references alike and base their operation on the average statistical observations. Some computers have dedicated cache(s) for instructions and/or data. The rest of this chapter (except for § 6.5) deals with alternatives to this organization.

6.1.2 Comparison of Registers and Caches for Scalars

The organization of the circular buffer of N register windows in the RISC architecture (§ 3.2) is such that the $N-1$ most recent procedure activation records are kept in that register file (except for the parts of activation records which do not fit in one register window). A cache memory of size M blocks, on the other hand, is organized so that the M most recently used memory blocks are kept in it. Since, in those organizations, procedure activation records are kept in a LIFO memory stack, it follows that those parts of the most recent activation records that have actually been used in the recent past are kept in the cache memory. Thus, a multi-window register file approximately holds a subset of what a cache memory holds, and both of those devices are fast memories intended to provide quick access to their contents. The similarities and the differences among the two approaches will be further investigated here.

A register file will hold *all* the local scalars of a procedure, or a random subset of them in the rare case where there are more than can fit into a window. A cache, on the other hand, will only hold those local scalars which have actually been used in the recent past. In this respect, the cache memory is better, since it adapts itself *dynamically* rather than statically to the demands of the computation. Two negative effects, however, make this adaptability worse than what it might be theoretically. First, whole *blocks* containing the most frequently used scalars are kept in the cache, not just the words themselves. This increases the probability that the precious on-chip memory locations hold unused data.

Second, most caches are set-associative with a small set-size. In that case, other data (or instructions) may overwrite some of the recently used local scalars. The difference in the adaptability of register files and caches is also reduced by the fact that most procedures have a few local scalars and use them heavily (§ 2.2.2), so that the static prediction is not far from the dynamic situation. On the other hand, fixed-size window schemes waste part of the window when the activation record is small (see next section).

At this point, it is worth discussing the issue of global scalars, as well. There are usually many global scalars, but only a few of them are heavily used. For example, *fgrep* (§ 2.4.1) has 20 global scalars declared, but only one of them is used in the critical loop. Cache memories will dynamically discover those variables and hold them. For a compiler, on the other hand, it is very difficult -- if not impossible -- to determine which ones are frequently used and to allocate them in registers. A viable approach requires the programmer to give hints to the compiler, using *register--type* declarations like the ones that C allows for local scalars. The same declarations would be useful for those few procedures which have more local scalars than a window can hold.

While the above comparisons did not show a decisive difference between a cache and a register file, these differ strongly when *addressing overhead* is considered. Caches offer addressing transparency at the machine-language level, at the expense of always referencing objects by their full, long identifier (address). Registers offer no such transparency at that level, but they allow referencing of objects by short identifiers. Addressing transparency for registers *is* offered in the HLL domain, which is all that matters for the programmer. The effect of the identifier size is very important, both in terms of accessing delay, and in terms of hardware requirements.

Figure 6.1.1 illustrates these points. To reference a local scalar in the RISC II multi-window register file, 8 bits of information are decoded in a specialized decoder, and one out of 138 registers is activated and places its contents onto the corresponding bus. To reference a local scalar on the execution stack, the stack-pointer *SP* must be selected and gated into an adder, where the short offset constant out of the instruction must be added to it. This is a *long addition* which produces a full-length memory address. The cache uses the LS-part of that address to access a wide RAM, in order to read a number of words and tags

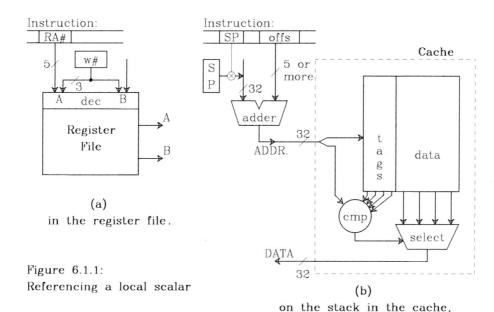

(a)
in the register file.

Figure 6.1.1:
Referencing a local scalar

(b)

on the stack in the cache.

equal to the set size. The MS-part of the address is compared to the tags, and one of the words that were read is selected.

It is clear that the long address addition required to access a local scalar on the stack makes such cache references slower than a register reference, even if the cache itself is equally fast as the register file. Pipelining can alleviate that, but the gains are limited by the occurrence of jump instructions. In most practical situations, the high cost of the hardware required to make cache references fast enough can not be afforded, and thus significant delays are introduced. Such examples are the following:

- The stack-pointer may be located in a general register file, thus requiring a register access for it to be read.
- Dedicated ALU's may not exist for computing the address of each of an instruction's two operands and for performing the arithmetic operations of the other instruction(s) in the pipeline.

- For a cache to be effective, it has to be larger than a multi-window register file (not counting tags), because it has to hold all kinds of data -- not just local scalars. This fact, combined with the tag comparison and word-selection, which are in series with RAM-reading, will normally make the cache access slower than a register access.
- A dual operand read-access to a dual-ported register file can be achieved with a register width equal to the word size. A 2-way set-associative cache, which is normally not dual-ported, requires that 4 words and 4 tags be read. Such large RAM widths may not be affordable for an on-chip cache.
- The communications bandwidth requirements are higher for the cache, due to the full-width memory address. This is an important bottleneck for off-chip caches.

The combined effects of the above points can be seen in the following table. It compares the speeds at which the PDP-11/70 and the VAX-11/780 can access local integers in their registers and in their cache:

	PDP-11/70	VAX-11/780
cache access time (hit)	300ns	200ns
register access time (μ-instr.)		200ns
i:=j; i,j: reg.	300ns	400ns
i:=j; i: reg., j: stack (hit).	1050ns	800ns
i:=j; i: stck (hit/write-thru), j: reg	1500ns	1200ns
i:=j; i,j: stack (hit/write-thru).	2250ns	1400ns

The superiority of multi-window register files over cache memories, for keeping scalar variables, is thus clear. There are two fundamental reasons for that. Firstly, scalars differ from data-structures in both their properties and their usage. Scalars are few, they are referenced repeatedly, and they are used to *name* data-structure elements (e.g. pointers, array-indexes). Secondly, when the sources of computations can conveniently be segregated into different storage devices, parallel access to them becomes possible. Such is the case with instructions, scalars, and data-structures.

6.2   Fixed-Size, Variable-Size, and Dribble-Back
Multi-Window Register Files

The RISC I and II register file organization has fixed-size windows, and copies these windows completely to/from memory when overflows or underflows occur (§ 3.2). That is not the only possible organization for a multi-window register file. Two alternative schemes are discussed in this section: register files with variable-size windows and "dribble-back" register files that save and restore windows "in the background" in parallel with normal instruction execution.

6.2.1 Variable-Size-Window Register Files

Allocating procedure arguments and local scalars into registers is possible, in the RISC window scheme, because the number of those scalars is quite small most of the time, and they can thus all fit into the current window. The measurements in [HaKe80] (§ 2.2.2) showed that the number of these arguments and locals is smaller than 13 in more than 95% of the executed procedure calls. The RISC II register file has enough space for 15 arguments and local scalars in each of its fixed-size windows (the 16th register is used for the return-PC).

While few of the procedures would need more registers than a window has, many of the procedures use only a few of the available registers in a window. According to the dynamic measurements in [HaKe80], a procedure activation record needs 4.6 ± 1.3 registers on the average for its arguments and locals. According to similar - but static - measurements in [DiML82], that number is 5.7 words per procedure on the average †. What this means is that a large portion of a fixed-size window remains unexploited most of the time, if that window is large enough for most of the activation records to fit in it. According to the above numbers, two thirds of the RISC II registers remain unutilized, on the average.

---

† Both measurements include all locals -- scalars and non-scalars. However, the averages given here only take into consideration those procedure activations which required ≤ 24 words for their arguments and locals, because it may safely be assumed that larger requirements arise only out of local non-scalars. The first number is the average of the 9 dynamic averages for the 9 measured programs. The second number is the average over the 1400 statically defined procedures in all of the standard UNIX commands (/usr/src/cmd/*.c).

Thus, sizable silicon resources are wasted; this is a serious drawback of the fixed-size window scheme.

The alternative is to use a register file with *variable-size* windows in which each window is only as large as is needed. Overall, such a register file needs fewer registers, because of the improved utilization. This has several desirable effects:

- transistors are freed and can be used for other functions on the chip,
- the register file is faster, due to its smaller size and correspondingly smaller parasitics (see [Sher84]), and
- saving and restoring registers into/from memory is faster, since no unused registers are copied.

Of course, a maximum window size is always imposed by the total register-file size and by the number of bits available in the instruction format for specifying a register-number. However, in this variable-window-size scheme, whenever a child procedure is called, the current window pointer only moves from its previous position by as many registers as the parent procedure actually uses, instead of moving by a fixed predefined distance. In this scheme, which is closer to the traditional stack of activation records, windows may "begin" (be aligned) on any arbitrary register in the register file. That means that the Current Window Pointer (*CWP*) must now have single-register resolution in pointing to the beginning of the current window. The register addressing process can no longer be done with a simple AND-OR decoder -- an addition must be performed, instead. Figure 6.2.1 illustrates these points. The required 6- or 7-bit adder in series with the register decoder will slow-down the decoding of register-numbers, which is on part of the critical path of the execution phase (fig. 4.2.1). Nevertheless, the delay of a carefully designed small adder needs not be much longer than the extra delay caused by the OR-AND-INVERT gates required for decoding the overlap registers in the fixed-size scheme (§ 4.2.3). This, coupled with the smaller and faster register file, may make the variable-size scheme quite attractive.

Another penalty that must be paid in the variable-size window scheme is the additional overhead per cali-return pair for updating the *CWP* and checking for overflows or underflows. These tasks cannot be carried out by hardwired decrement/increment and compare operations as in RISC II. Instead, the number

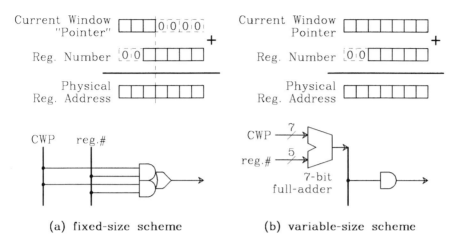

(a) fixed-size scheme   (b) variable-size scheme

Figure 6.2.1:   Register Decoders for Multi-Window Schemes (concept and implementation).

to be subtracted or added to *CWP*, and the distance of *CWP* from *SWP* to be checked for over/under-flow detection, depend on the number of arguments and locals of the parent or child procedures. These pairs of procedures may be separately compiled, in languages like C, and thus their respective requirements are not known at compilation time. Either the linkage editor should be used to patch the call/return statements, or an additional instruction per call-return pair is required. Figure 6.2.2 shows two of the available options for updating and checking *CWP* in the variable-size scheme.

• In (a), *CWP* points to the base (the ''beginning'') of the current window. When a parent calls a child, *CWP* is changed by the size of the parent's frame, and availability is checked for a maximum-size new window. These can both be performed by the *call* instruction. When the child returns, *CWP* has to be changed by the size of the *parent's* frame again. However, that size is not known to the child procedure which executes the *return* instruction, unless the linkage editor patches the code. In the absence of such patching, an extra instruction has to be inserted after each

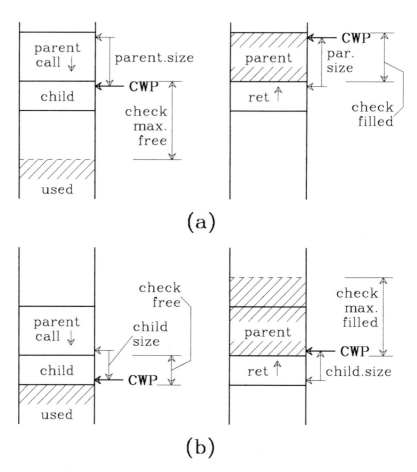

Figure 6.2.2: Update-&-Check Options
with Variable-Size Scheme.

call, to "catch" the return, to update *CWP*, and to check whether the parent's registers are still present in the register file. Alternatively, the parent's *CWP* value may be passed to the child along with the return-*PC*.

- Part (b) of figure 6.2.2 shows the second option, in which the *CWP* points to the "limit" of the current window. In that case, *CWP* has to be changed by the size of the child's frame upon calls and returns. When the *return* instruction is executed, that size is known, and no problem exists (the check for validity of the parent's registers is made for the maximum possible size of the parent's frame). However, the *call* instruction is executed by the parent, and thus an extra instruction has to be inserted at the entrance of the child procedure. This scheme inserts statically less extra instructions (dynamically both schemes execute the same number of extra instructions), but when the child checks for free space it must check for the sum of its own frame plus the maximum number of outgoing arguments of all of its *call*'s. With this scheme, passing the parent's *CWP* along with the return-*PC* does not work.

• A third option, used in Ditzel's C Machine Register-Stack [DiML82], is to insert extra instructions both at the entry-point of every procedure and at the target of every *return* instruction. In this way, an accurate check for over/under-flow is possible on both call's and return's.

Ditzel's "Stack Cache Register Set" for the C Machine, described in [DiML82], is similar to the variable-size window scheme, except that the *CWP* is extended to be a full 32-bit memory address. In that way, registers are always accessed with their equivalent memory address. To avoid the high penalty of performing the long addition *CWP + offset* once per register access, that addition is performed at the time the instruction is fetched into the instruction cache. This scheme exploits the statistical fact that many of the non-recursive procedures are called with the same *CWP* many or all the times. When this is not the case (with recursive procedures for example), the procedure code is re-fetched into the cache upon the new procedure activation. The accessing of the registers with memory addresses makes this scheme be quite similar to a cache memory (§ 6.1.2). Its fundamental difference from a cache is that it is only used for the top of the execution stack. In this way, parallel access to it and to the rest of the memory is possible, and it is managed as a single circular buffer with no address tags, no LRU replacement, and no set-associativity.

6.2.2 Dribble-Back Register Files

In the multi-window schemes that were examined up to now, saving and restoring windows to/from memory was only done on overflows and underflows respectively. These schemes are successful when enough windows exist, so that overflows and underflows rarely occur. An alternative scheme is to perform the saving and restoring *before* a need for it arises and to perform it *"in the background"*, that is, in parallel with normal instruction execution. As long as this background copying does not slow down program execution, it doesn't matter how frequently windows are saved or restored. Thus, it is possible to have very few windows in a register file that is managed with this method. This kind of management was proposed by Sites in [Site79], who used the name "dribble-back" to describe it.

The advantage of a dribble-back register file is that it can be small in size, and thus fast in operation ([Sher84]). Also, in the ideal case, it will never overflow or underflow. Its disadvantage is the high memory bandwidth which it requires for saving/restoring registers in parallel with normal instruction execution. Thus, dribble-back register files are attractive for high-performance systems, where the cost of the extra bandwidth may be affordable. To provide sufficient bandwidth, one might use a pipelined cache that permits two accesses per machine cycle -- one for the executing instruction and one for the saving/restoring process. Alternatively, separate instruction and data caches may be utilized. In processors employing register windows, the data-memory-port is often left idle. In the measurements reported in § 3.2.2, only about one fifth of all executed RISC instructions were *load* or *store*. The idle memory cycles can be used in the background for saving or restoring registers.

Figure 6.2.3 shows a dribble-back register file with two windows -- the minimum possible size.

(a) shows a data-movement organization selected for ease of understanding the operation of the scheme. Upon execution of a *call* instruction, the local and input-argument registers of the parent procedure are copied (saved) into a back-up set of registers (window). Simultaneously, the output-argument registers are copied into the input-argument ones. Now, the child procedure can start executing, with its input arguments in the input-registers, and with the local and output registers free to be used. In parallel with the child's

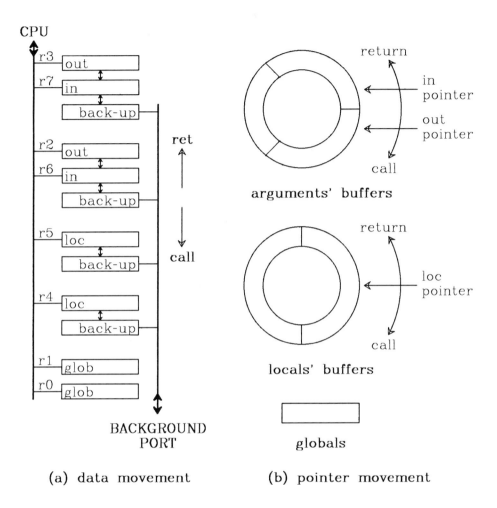

Figure 6.2.3:   Dribble-Back Register File.

execution, the back-up window is copied (saved) to memory, in preparation for the event of another *call* occurrence. If that other *call* does not occur, then upon execution of the *return* instruction by the child, the input-registers are copied into the output-registers, thus returning values to the parent, and the back-up set of registers is copied into the local and input registers, thus restoring the parent's activation record. Now, in parallel with the parent procedure continuing execution, the back-up window must be prepared for the event of another *return* instruction; the locals and input-arguments of the grand-parent must be copied (restored) from memory into those back-up registers.

Thus, the following management schedule is followed: After a *call* instruction, prepare for a new *call* by saving the parent's frame. After a *return* instruction, prepare for a new *return* by restoring the parent's frame.

Part (b) of figure 6.2.3 shows an organization that is preferable for implementation. Here, pointers are changed, instead of moving data from one window into another. In this organization each register cell only needs connections to the CPU bus(es) and to the background-port bus. In organization (a), register cells need connection to one less bus, but they need additional *shift-type* connections to their neighbours. These shift-type connections are more expensive than normal bus connections in terms of silicon area; thus register-file (b) is more compact than file (a). Another disadvantage of organization (a) is that all registers are copied on *call/return*'s, thus requiring extra power for data transfer. For this reason, organization (b) was also preferred for the RISC register file.

The main advantage of dribble-back register files is their smaller physical size, resulting from the low number of windows required. Successful performance of the minimum-size dribble-back register file is critically dependent on whether enough time is usually available between two successive procedure calls for a window to be saved in memory, and between two successive procedure returns for a window to be restored from memory. To evaluate this, the profiled code of the *sed* and *mextra* programs (see § 2.4.2 and § 2.4.4) was analyzed by hand, yielding the following dynamic measurements:

- When procedures are called and start executing:
    - ≈ 1/2 of them call no further children;
    - ≈ 1/3 of them call another procedure after executing 0 to 4 HLL statements (that is 0 to 10 machine instructions); and
    - the remaining ≈ 1/6 of them call another procedure after executing 6 to 10 HLL statements.

- After a child returns to its parent:
  - in 50 or 70 % of the cases, another procedure is called in a while;
  - in 35 or 10 % of the cases, the parent returns after executing 0 to 1 HLL statements ($\approx$ 0 to 3 machine instructions); and
  - in 15 or 20 % of the cases, the parent returns after executing 4 or more HLL statements.

These numbers mean that, with a 2-window dribble-back register file, roughly 30% of the calls or returns will have to wait because the back-up window is not yet ready -- unless the background-coping memory port has a bandwidth of *several* words per machine cycle. Thus, effective multi-window register files with very few windows are not easily achieved with the dribble-back scheme.

6.3   Support for Fast Instruction Fetching and Sequencing

The process of fetching instructions performs two basic functions:
- supplying "fuel" -- i.e. instructions -- to the execution unit, in order for the computation to proceed, and
- guiding the computation onto the proper path, according to decisions dynamically made in the execution unit.

In a high-performance processor, where simple instructions control a pipelined data-path, it is important for both of these functions to be fast. This section investigates hardware and architectural support for achieving that goal.

The various organizations proposed in this section are centered around the use of an instruction cache. As mentioned in the introduction of this chapter, an instruction cache is one of the desirable hardware enhancements for a high-performance processor, for several reasons:

- a cache for instructions is an effective device, because it exploits the locality of references arising out of loops in programs;

- a cache that is dedicated to instructions is simpler than a general cache, because it is read-only;

- an instruction cache which is separate from the data-memory port of the CPU is desirable for allowing parallel instruction and data accesses (§ 3.3.2);

- an on-chip instruction cache utilizes the silicon area more effectively than microcode ROM, because it dynamically adapts its contents to the requirements of the executing program.

- an independent instruction cache lends itself to incorporation into an instruction fetch-and-sequence unit (see below).

An alternative to an instruction cache is a single or multiple instruction buffer. Such buffers are simpler than a general cache and rely on the usual small size of critical loops. However, the effectiveness of buffer schemes is limited by the fact that each iteration of a critical loop often consists of the execution of several small *non-contiguous* blocks of instructions, rather than of a single contiguous block that could fit in an instruction buffer. As an example, the small critical loop of *fgrep* (§ 2.4.1), which consists of the execution of only 11 lines of source code, actually extends over two pages of source program. Since about one out of 4 to 6 executed instructions is a successful conditional branch or call/return, the average size of blocks of contiguously executed instructions is only about 4 to 6 instructions (see § 6.3.2, § 2.2.1).

6.3.1 Remote-PC Instruction Units

The instruction fetching process enjoys a significant degree of independence from the computation process. That independence is the basis of a desirable hardware partitioning into separate fetching and execution units, allowing for both locality of information processing and parallelism of operation.

Figure 6.3.1 shows an organization that minimizes the communication bandwidth between an instruction fetch-&-sequence unit and the unit which executes instructions. The Program Counter (PC) is contained in the former unit, hence the name *"remote-PC"* scheme. The fetch-&-sequence unit understands and executes control-transfer instructions -- jumps, calls, and returns. For that unit, two characteristics of the instruction sequencing mode are important:

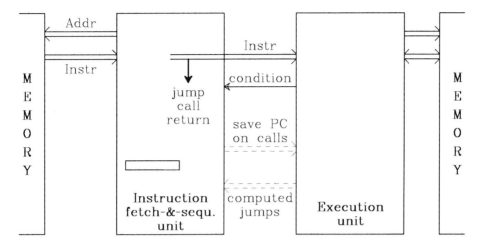

Figure 6.3.1:   Remote-PC Scheme.

- *Conditional/Unconditional Sequencing:* For conditional transfer instructions, a 1-bit condition -- supplied by the execution-unit -- selects one of two possible paths. For unconditional sequencing, a single path is possible, whether it be a linear (no transfers), or a non-linear (unconditional transfer) one.

- *Static/Dynamic Transfer Target:* The address of the instruction to-be-executed-next is usually known statically at compile time and thus does *not* depend on the execution-unit. Exceptions are the *return* instructions and the infrequent "computed jumps" (e.g. for *case* statements).

The average communication bandwidth between a remote-PC instruction-unit and the execution-unit is not much more than the minimum bandwidth needed to merely supply the instructions to the execution unit. That is so because addresses are transmitted infrequently between the two units. Control transfers with a dynamic target are not very frequent (return instructions are less than 5% of all executed RISC instructions [PaSe81]). Also, the jump instructions do not need to be sent to the execution unit. The bandwidth achieved in this way is significantly lower than the one required in the conventional scheme, where the *PC* is kept in the execution unit and has to be sent out of it for every single instruction-fetch. This low bandwidth shows that information is maintained and processed locally to a maximum degree; this makes such a partitioning desirable.

In order for the remote-PC implementation to be successful, the value of *PC* should be used as little as possible in the execution of instructions. In particular, no PC-relative addressing mode should exist for data accesses (see § 3.1.2). An instruction-unit with remote-PC and with an instruction cache, will be the basis for the hardware enhancements proposed in the rest of this section. The Instruction-Cache chip that was designed and built for RISC II [Patt83] does include a remote-PC; however, the latter contains only an estimated value of the real *PC*, and is used for predictive fetching of instructions. The RISC II CPU was *not* designed for a remote-PC system, and thus it includes the *PC* in itself, and it has PC-relative *load* and *store* instructions.

6.3.2 Jumps, and Delays Introduced by them

An instruction fetch-&-sequence unit has to deal efficiently with control-transfer instructions, because they occur very frequently. The following table reviews some of the measurements presented in § 2.2.1:

Property:	Measurement:	Reference:
Opcodes, dynamically:		
branching instructions	30 %	[Lund77]
branch instruction	14 %	[AlWo75]
uncond. jumps, rel. to all jumps	55 %	[AlWo75]
HLL statements statically:		
if	13 %	[AlWo75]
call	13 %	[AlWo75]

HLL statements dynamically:

if	36 % ± 15 %	[PaSe82]
call	14 % ± 4 %	[PaSe82]
loops	4 % ± 3 %	[PaSe82]
call	12 %	[Tane78]

These numbers show the validity of the commonly used rule of thumb that "one out of four executed instructions is a control-transfer". The following program fragment out of § 2.4.4 is quite typical of non-numeric programs, as far as frequency of jumps is concerned, and illustrates the same point:

```
| while(new != NIL && old != NIL)            /* NIL is 0 */
|    { if(new→bb.l < old→bb.l) { infrequent }
|      else { if(n < old→bb.t)
|                  { if(last == NIL) { rare }
|                    else { last→next = old; last = old; }
|                    old = oldList;
|                    if(old != NIL) oldList = old→next;
|                  }
|            else { infrequent }
|          }
|      if(depth[last→layer] == 0) {50% of the times: call a proc.}
|      if((depth[last→layer] += last→dir) == 0) {again: 50% call}
|      nextEnd = (nextEnd < last→bb.t ? nextEnd : last→bb.t);
|    }
```

Besides illustrating the high frequency of *jump* instructions, the above program fragment also shows the intimate connection between *jumps* and *test* or *compare* instructions. The usual pattern is that a number is compared to zero (*test*), or two numbers are compared to each other (*compare*), and a conditional jump is then executed, based on the outcome of the comparison. Hennessy et.al. studied how many of the conditional jumps require an explicit comparison operation performed for their sake and how many of them can use the result of some other instruction [Henn82, table 2.3]. They measured that less than 2% of the conditional jumps were able to use condition-codes set by an instruction that was *not* executed solely for that purpose.

Fast control-transfer instructions are particularly important for high processor performance, because they are so frequent and because they block the fetch-execute pipeline. This importance becomes even more significant when the combined time spent for branches *and* comparisons is considered. For that reason, the rest of this section will focus on fast *compare—and—branch* operations.

6.3.3 Fast Compare-and-Branch Scheme

Figure 6.3.2(a) shows the compare-and-branch scheme followed in RISC I & II. Given that in about half of the cases the optimizer is able to move something useful into the cycle labeled "OTHER", we can say that this scheme takes about 2.5 cycles, on average, for a comparison and a branch.

There are two possibilities for improvement of this scheme. First, the comparison and the decision whether to take the branch or not can be executed in parallel with the computation of the possible branch target, PC+offset. This would require two ALU's, but it would reduce the time for a compare-and-branch to about 1.5 cycles. This scheme comes only natural when a separate instruction fetch-and-sequence unit is used, like the one of § 6.3.1. Second, the branch target address is known at compile time, and there is no reason -- other than code compactness -- why it should be recomputed every time the branch is executed. When an instruction cache is used, a solution exists that allows both the code to be compact and the target address computation not to slow down the instruction-fetching. It will be presented in the next subsection 6.3.4.

Figure 6.3.2(b) shows the proposed fast compare-&-branch scheme. It makes use of both of the above improvements, and it allows single-cycle compare-&-branch instructions. However, now there is not enough time for the jump/no-jump decision to be made before the fetching of the target instruction begins. Thus, a two-port instruction cache is required, that fetches simultaneously both possible targets of the conditional branch.

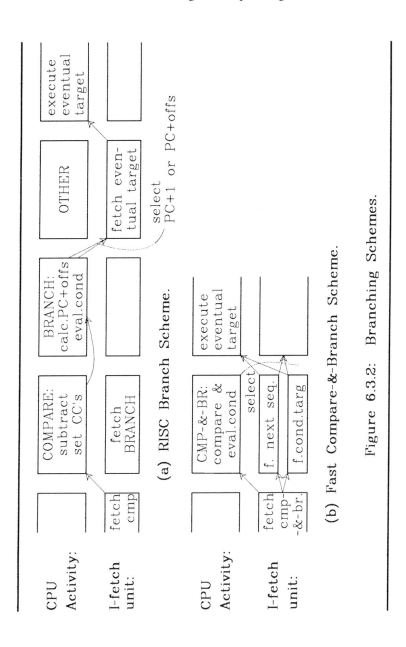

(a) RISC Branch Scheme.

(b) Fast Compare-&-Branch Scheme.

Figure 6.3.2: Branching Schemes.

6.3.4 Target Address Specification for Fast-Branching

Most branches have a target not very far from the branch itself. Some measurements for a particular language and architecture have shown 55% of the branches targeted within a distance of 128 bytes, or 93% of them targeted within a 16 Kbytes range (see § 2.2.1 [AlWo75]). This locality property is the basis of the familiar PC-relative branch instruction, which achieves high code density by specifying the target's *distance* from the branch. Figure 6.3.3(a) illustrates this method. In that figure, thick lines represent information statically determined (by the compiler) and thus included in the instruction. Thin lines represent dynamically computed information. In the traditional PC-relative branch scheme, shown in (a), the instruction contains a $(n+1)$-bit *offset* field, which is added to the PC at execution time and produces the conditional target address. All branches to within a distance of $\pm 2^n$ from the current instruction can be represented with this instruction format (see the little graph on the right).

The rest of figure 6.3.3 shows three variants of the proposed alternative fast-branching scheme. The key idea here is that the instruction contains the n least-significant (LS) bits of the *conditional target address* itself, rather than of its *offset*. In this way, the instruction cache can start fetching that target as soon as the branch instruction becomes known to it, without having to wait for the result of an n-bit addition. This approach assumes that the block address of the cache is not wider than n bits. The most-significant (MS) part of the conditional target address still has to be computed at execution time, assuming a compact branch instruction that cannot contain the whole address. However, this computation can be performed in parallel with the cache RAM access, as long as its result becomes available in time for the address tag comparison. There are three different ways in which the MS part of the conditional target address can be computed in the fast-branch scheme, and they are illustrated in parts (b), (c), and (d) of fig. 6.3.3.

The straightforward transformation of the traditional scheme (a) into the fast-branch scheme is shown in (b). The sign-bit of the *offset* and the carry-bit from the (virtual) n-LS-bit addition are computed by the compiler and included in the instruction, so that the MS part of the same addition can be recreated. This scheme requires an $(n+2)$-bit instruction-field for specifying the conditional target, and it achieves a worst-case branching range of $\pm 2^n$.

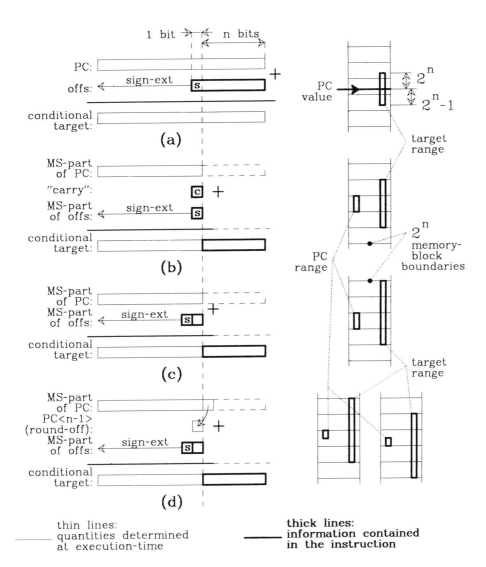

Figure 6.3.3: Avoiding the LS-part
of the addition to determine the conditional
target of a PC-relative branch.

The second variant shown in (c) is better than that of (b). The compiler supplies again 2 bits of information for computing the MS part of the conditional target address. However, instead of adding *both* of them to bit $<n>$ of PC as in (b), they are considered as forming a 2-bit signed number which is added to the MS part of PC. This achieves a worst-case branching range of -2^{n+1} to $+2^{n}$. The scheme in (d) is similar to that in (c). It uses the $PC<n-1>$ bit as a round-off bit to achieve an equally balanced worst-case branching range of $\pm 1.5 \times 2^{n}$.

Figure 6.3.4 shows the block diagram of an instruction fetch-and-sequence unit that incorporates a two-port instruction cache and the fast compare-and-branch scheme. (This is the simple form of the I-unit; figure 6.3.6 shows the full form.) The double register $\{PCplus\,1, Instruction\ Register\}$ at the CPU interface is loaded at the beginning of each execution cycle with the instruction to be executed and with its incremented PC value. The incremented-PC value is used as the address for one of the two instruction-cache ports, and causes the subsequent instruction to be fetched. Simultaneously, the appropriate field of the current instruction -- assuming that this is a branch -- is used for determining a possible target-address, according to the scheme of fig. 6.3.3 (c) or (d). This possible target-address is fed to the second port of the instruction cache, and a possible target-instruction is fetched. At the end of the cycle, the execution unit has decided whether this was a conditional branch, and whether it should be taken or not. According to that decision, the multiplexors IRMUX and PCMUX select the output of the first or second cache port and the output of the first or second address incrementer, in order to load the instruction- and the incremented-PC registers. Notice that the instruction cache should *not* initiate the miss-process before it is certain that the offending access is for an instruction that will actually be executed. The next subsection looks at the timing of compare-&-branch instructions in more detail.

6.3.5 Form of Comparisons in the Fast-Branch Scheme

Figure 6.3.5 is a graph of the timing-dependencies for the compare-&-branch instruction. It is similar to the one in figure 4.2.1, and it assumes a processor with a data-path similar to that of RISC II and with the fast-branch I-unit of fig. 6.3.4. The points labeled A, B, and C on this graph correspond to the similarly labeled points in fig. 6.3.4. At point A, an instruction is ready to start executing. Assume that it is a compare-&-branch instruction that has to perform a

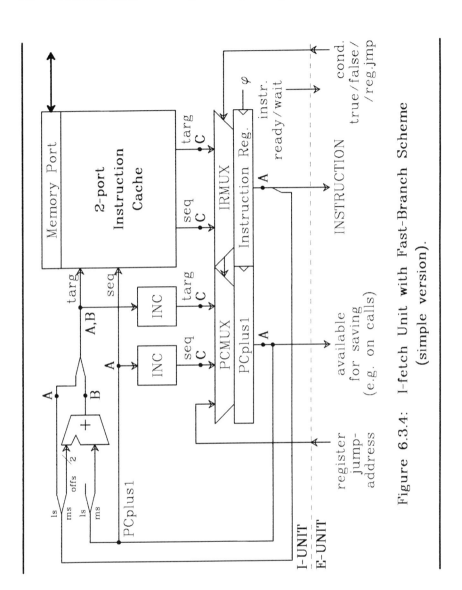

Figure 6.3.4: I-fetch Unit with Fast-Branch Scheme (simple version).

comparison in the execution-unit (upper cycle), while the I-unit fetches its two possible successor instructions (lower cycle). The n LS bits of the addresses of both candidate successors are known at point A (see figures 6.3.4 and 6.3.3(c,d)). Thus, the cache RAM access can begin immediately. (We assume that n bits are enough to address the words and the blocks of the cache RAM). The cache RAM access is complete at point B, at which point the MS part of the conditional-target must also have been computed. The cache tag comparison may begin at point B and must be completed at point C when the next instruction is ready to be selected. At the same point C, the two incrementers INC (fig. 6.3.4) must have valid outputs; notice that the carry of the second INC propagates in parallel with the carry of the target-address addition.

At the same point C, the execution-unit must have decided whether the branch should be taken or not, so that the next instruction can be selected. Assuming an instruction set and a data-path similar to those of RISC II, the compare-&-branch instruction must decode two registers (A→D), must read them from the register-file (D→E), and must compare them and decide (E→C). This comparison may or may not require a subtraction. Figure 6.3.5 clearly shows that it would be overly restrictive for the data-path to leave enough time between points E and C for a full-width subtraction. The reason is that all other instructions may allow almost a full cycle E→F for the ALU operation. (See fig. 4.2.1; however, here, we do *not* want the ALU to be on the I-fetch critical path.) Thus, the possible forms of the comparison should be restricted, so that *no subtraction* is required.

This means that comparisons to zero ("tests") can be allowed, as well as comparisons of two arbitrary quantities for equality or inequality. None of those requires a circuit with carry-propagation for its detection -- they are resolved by just looking at the most significant bit of the source or by using a wide precharged NOR gate to check for equality to zero, possibly after computing a bitwise exclusive-OR in the ALU. However, a magnitude comparison of two arbitrary quantities should not be allowed in a compare-&-branch instruction, since it requires an adder or a priority encoder for its implementation.

This restricted comparison form is another example of an architectural decision made for implementation reasons. To evaluate its effects in real programs, the critical program fragments presented in sections 2.3 and 2.4 were analyzed by hand.

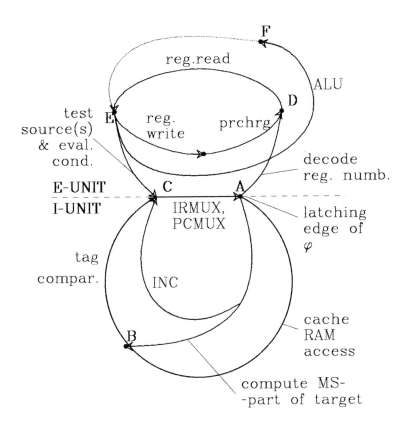

Figure 6.3.5: Timing Dependencies
in Proposed Compare-&-Branch Scheme.

All comparisons for conditional branches were classified into four categories:

- TST: arbitrary comparisons to zero;
- EQ/NE: comparison of two quantities for equality/inequality;
- CMP-SOFT: those comparison used for deciding the termination of a DO-loop, which are of the form $if\ (i \geq LIMIT)$, and which could be rewritten in the form $if\ (i == LIMIT)$;
- CMP-HARD: all comparisons of two arbitrary quantities for $>$, $\geq$, $<$, $\leq$, and which are not CMP-SOFT.

They were counted dynamically; the average percentages in each type of comparison are given below, separately for the 17 numeric critical loops (§ 2.3), and for the 3 non-numeric programs (*fgrep, sed, mextra*: § 2.4):

	TST	EQ/NE	CMP-SOFT	CMP-HARD
numeric programs	18 % ±32	13 % ±23	51 % ±43	18 % ±28
non-num. prog.	55 % ±11	24 % ±8	6 % ±8	15 % ±15

These numbers show that, with no program re-writing, the restricted-form comparisons would be useful in about 40% of the cases for numeric programs and in about 80% of the cases for non-numeric ones. With program re-writing or with language semantics that allow equality comparison in DO-loops, these numbers would become about 80% and about 85%, respectively. Thus, the restricted comparison form appears quite frequently in real programs, especially in non-numeric ones.

From the point of view of the instruction format, the compare-&-branch instruction *can* fit in 32 bits, although certainly not in a fashion compatible with the RISC I & II instruction format. This incompatibility may result in performance penalties due to a more complicated instruction decoding, if this scheme is used within an ISP like that of the Berkeley RISC. A possible set of instruction-fields and widths for that instruction is the following:

- 3-bit opcode,
- 4-bit branch-condition specifier and $S2$ selector,
- 5-bit R_{s1} specifier,
- 8-bit $S2$: R_{s2} or a byte-wide immediate,
- 12-bit target-address specifier ($n = 10$ in fig. 6.3.3).

The 12-bit target-address specifier allows the use of 10-bit addresses for the cache RAM. This corresponds to a maximum cache size of 2 K-instructions for a 2-way associative cache, or 4 K-instructions for a 4-way associative one, which are reasonable limits.

6.3.6 Extension for Zero-Delay Unconditional Branches

Figure 6.3.6 shows the full version of an instruction fetch-and-sequence unit with a two-port instruction cache. This version, besides implementing the fast compare-&-branch scheme of § 6.3.3, also executes unconditional branches in "zero-time", i.e. without holding the execution-unit while it follows those branches. An exception are unconditional branches which follow conditional ones within a distance of 1 or 2 instructions: they *will* hold the execution unit for 1 cycle.

As we saw in § 6.3.2, about half of all branches are unconditional, thus accounting for roughly 1/10 of all executed instructions. They arise in a natural way when the non-linear flow-diagram of a program is converted into machine-code stored in a linear memory. Unconditional branches describe no useful computation; they just divert the instruction-fetching process onto a different path. It is interesting to note that unconditional branches are usually "for free" in micro-code since micro-instructions usually contain the address of their successor inside themselves. The same general scheme can also be used with macro instructions.

A two-port instruction cache is used for simultaneously fetching both possible targets of compare-&-branch instructions. The basic idea behind the full version of the I-unit is to also exploit both ports of the instruction-cache when instructions other than compare-&-branch are executing. When such an "other" instruction is executing, the $PCplus\,1$ and $PCplus\,2$ registers are used to fetch its next *two* instructions, say I_{S1} and I_{S2}. If I_{S2} is an unconditional branch, and I_{S1} is neither an unconditional nor a conditional one, then I_{S1} can be supplied to the E-unit for normal execution, and the target address of I_{S2} can be followed *immediately*. While I_{S1} is being executed in the E-unit, the *target* of I_{S2} is fetched; and the unconditional branch becomes invisible to the execution unit.

Unconditional branches can have an instruction-format different from that of conditional ones. This makes possible the immediate pursuit of the target address without the need for techniques similar to those of the fast compare-&-branch scheme (§ 6.3.4). Unconditional branches can have a 3-bit opcode and a 29-bit absolute target address. It is advantageous to make the target of all unconditional branches be an even-word aligned instruction. In that way, both the target instruction and the instruction next to the target can be fetched by concatenating

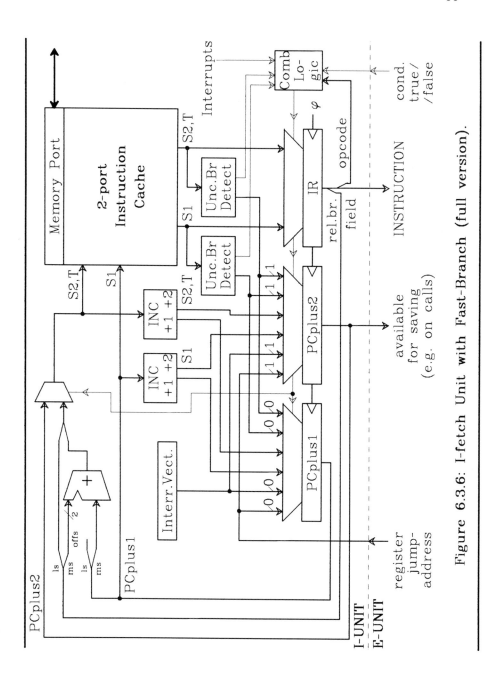

Figure 6.3.6: I-fetch Unit with Fast-Branch (full version).

the 29-bit target-field with ''000'' and with ''100'' (byte addresses), respectively. These quantities are fed to *PCplus* 1 and *PCplus* 2 as soon as I_{S2} is detected to be an unconditional branch. This format for unconditional branches also offers a means of branching to arbitrarily distant memory locations, unlike the restricted-range compare-&-branch instructions.

Call instructions perform the same function as do unconditional branches do, except that they must also save the *PC* for use upon procedure return. If the place to save the *PC* is a fixed register in the child's window, then *call* instructions can have the same format of a 3-bit opcode and a 29-bit absolute target address. The I-unit can treat *calls* similar to unconditional branches, except that it must also supply them to the E-unit, which must execute them by saving the *PC*.

Normally, an unconditional branch should first appear as the second one of the two consecutive instructions I_{S1} and I_{S2} being fetched from memory locations $M[PCplus1]$ and $M[PCplus2]$, respectively. The reason is that, if execution has been sequential in the recent past, then an unconditional branch fetched via $M[PCplus1]$ would also have been fetched via $M[PCplus2]$ one cycle earlier and would have been executed at that time. That will not happen if execution has not been sequential in the recent past, and specificly if an unconditional branch is the target of another one or if it follows a compare-&-branch within a distance of 1 or 2 instructions. (Notice that occurrences of the former situation can be removed by the optimizer or the linkage editor.) Because these cases have to be dealt with, unconditional branches should also be detected and handled when appearing at the first ($S1$) port of the I-cache. However, in those cases there is nothing else useful that can be supplied to the E-unit while the target of the branch is being fetched. Thus, the unconditional branch itself can be given to the E-unit, which should interpret it as a *noop*.

In this section, instruction fetch-and-sequence units of increasing sophistication have been proposed. When sufficient hardware resources are available for the implementation of such an I-unit, a high-performance execution-unit can be kept busy and the time spent executing control-transfer instructions can be reduced. Roughly 1.5 cycles per conditional branch and one cycle per unconditional branch can be saved, amounting to about 2.5 cycles out of every 10 cycles of execution.

6.4   Pointers and Data Caches

According to the list of proposed priorities at the beginning of this chapter, hardware resources that remain available after a multi-window register file and an instruction-unit have been implemented, should be spent for a data cache. The two former devices were investigated in the previous sections. In this section, the special nature of accesses to non-scalar data is considered as far as the construction of an effective data cache is concerned, and hardware as well as programming methods for its exploitation are proposed.

6.4.1 Data-Structure Accesses and Data Caches

Operands used by programs are either scalar variables or elements of non-scalar data-structures. These two categories differ fundamentally, as pointed out in § 6.1.1. Scalars are few in number, they occupy little memory space, they are referenced using their own name, and several of them are used repeatedly. They are often used to refer to particular elements of data-structures. Data-structures, on the other hand, have many elements and occupy large memory space. Individual elements of these structures are accessed via dynamically computed addresses.

Accesses to non-scalars follow certain typical patterns:

A • A number of *repeated accesses to the same element* is often made before interest shifts to another element of the data-structure. For example, $A[i,j]$ is accessed three times during each critical-loop iteration in fig. 2.3.1; the element *last−>layer* is accessed ≈ 4 times per iteration in the procedure **ScanSubSwath()** in § 2.4.4. Another, less frequent, case arises in the critical loop of **fgrep** in fig. 2.4.1. The pointer c is pointing to the same element of the structure *words* during most loop iterations, because the scanner is searching for the same first letter of the desired pattern most of the time.

B • *Accesses to near-by memory locations* are frequently made. They arise in two different ways. First, arrays are frequently traversed in a sequential manner such that each element accessed is next to the previously visited one, in terms of its memory address. This is true for sequential scanning of linear arrays (character buffer scanning is a common case), as well as for the scanning of multi-dimensional arrays *by columns* (in FORTRAN). These occur quite frequently (see § 2.3, 2.4.1, 2.4.2). Second, more than one of the fields of a structure are usually accessed before program execution moves to another structure (§ 2.4.4). Since structures are often small in size, their fields are in near-by memory locations. To evaluate that size, static measurements were collected (by hand) on the size of the structure types declared in 15 C programs, including a screen editor (emacs), a HLL interpreter (logo), *fgrep*, *sed*, and *mextra*. Among 54 structure declarations investigated, about 45% of them were found to have 4 or less words; about 70% had 8 or less words; and about 85% had 16 or less words. All sizes are for the VAX-11/780, where 1 word equals 4 bytes.

C • However, the occasional *shift of accesses to remote locations* can not be neglected. It occurs whenever array accesses are not sequential in address space, or when various nodes of dynamically allocated data-structured are accessed. The former case is not very frequent for linear arrays, but it is common for multi-dimensional ones. The latter case occurs due to the "random" allocation in memory of nodes that are linked to each other. In practical situations, however, this allocation is not completely random, and some linked nodes do end up next to each other. A study of 5 large LISP programs by Clark and Green [ClGr77], for example, showed that about 1/4 of the *car* and *cdr* list pointers were pointing to the immediately adjacent (forward direction) memory cell.

Registers are the natural device for holding frequently used scalars, because of the small number and size of those variables. A cache memory, on the other hand, is well suited for keeping the elements of data structures, because of access patterns A and B above. The fact that caches keep the most recently used words in them accelerates type-A accesses, while the fact that caches fetch a whole block when a word is missed accelerates type-B accesses.

A data-cache, that is separate from the instruction-fetch port of the CPU, can allow one-cycle *load* and *store* instructions in the RISC II architecture and pipeline. A timing scheme similar to that of fig. 3.3.4(b) is used for that purpose, except that here no restriction needs to be placed on the RISC II addressing mode $R_d \leftarrow \rightarrow M[R_{s1}+S2]$. Figure 6.4.1 shows the timing of a *load* instruction when a data-cache is used. The data-cache access may begin just a little while after the addressing addition has started in the ALU. The reason is that only the least-significant bits of the effective address $R_{s1}+S2$ are required for the cache RAM

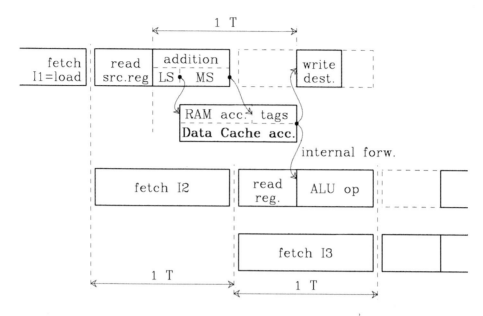

Figure 6.4.1: One-Cycle Load Instructions
in a RISC II with a Data-Cache.

access. The rest of the bits of the effective address are needed later on when the
address tag comparison takes place. Internal forwarding allows the next instruction $I2$ to use the loaded data. For a cache that requires the n LS address bits for
its RAM access, the timing constraint is:

$$(Data\ Cache\ Access\ Time) \le T - (n-bit\ Add\ Time).$$

Notice that for this scheme to be possible, the data-cache needs to be separate
from the instruction-fetch port of the CPU (e.g. the instruction-cache), so that the
required parallel access to both of them is possible.

Cache misses limit overall performance. Accesses of type C cause misses,
and so do those of type B when they cross block boundaries. The next subsection proposes hardware and programming methods for reducing the number of
those misses.

6.4.2 Pointers as Pre-Fetching Hints

There is an intimate connection between pointers and data-structure accesses. Most accesses to fields of structures are made indirectly through a pointer scalar variable that is pointing to the structure, and most of those pointer variables are local ones. Similarly, in non-numeric programs, array accesses are often made using pointers to the array elements such as character-buffer accesses in text-processing programs. For example, 85 % of the accesses to non-scalar data made in the critical loops in § 2.4 have the form $*p$ or $p \rightarrow fld$, where p is a local scalar variable; the remaining 15 % of those accesses have the forms $arr[n]$ or $(non-scalar) \rightarrow fld$ †. In numeric programs, array accesses are traditionally made using subscripts (in languages like FORTRAN this is the only choice). These, however, could also be replaced by indirections through local pointers by the optimizer or by the sophisticated programmer, as noted in § 2.3.4. Such a replacement would simplify the required address computations, and would also make forthcoming proposals applicable to these accesses as well.

When a scalar pointer variable is loaded with a new value, it is very likely for that value to be used shortly afterwards for an indirect access to an array element or to a field of a structure. For example, after 90 % of the assignments to a local pointer p made in the critical loops in § 2.4, the assigned value was used for an access of the type $*p$ or $p \rightarrow fld$. These accesses are always made to the memory word where p is pointing to ($*p$), or to neighbouring words ($p \rightarrow fld$). In the remaining 10 % of the cases, p was used for purposes other than indirect memory accesses -- for example it was compared to a limit value †.

This suggests that a data cache should use the assignment of a value to a pointer variable as a *hint for prefetching* into the cache the block where this pointer is pointing to, if it is not already there. In this way, some of the type-C accesses (§ 6.4.1) may be turned into type-A or type-B ones, and the miss ratio may be reduced. In a processor where registers are used to hold the most frequently used scalar variables, the criterion for prefetching a block into the data cache may simply be the writing of a pointer value into a register. One way of distinguishing pointer from non-pointer assignments is by setting aside some registers for pointer values only (''index registers''). This, however, reduces the

---

† These measurements are static; however, they were collected only from critical loops (§ 2.4).

flexibility and orthogonality of the architecture and leads to non-optimal utilization of the register file. A better way is to have the compiler tell the machine, with one bit in the instruction, that the assigned value is a pointer one. The proposed prefetching scheme is reminiscent of the way loads and stores are performed on the CDC-6600 computer [Thor64]; a memory-to-data-register transaction is implicitly initiated every time an address-register is loaded with a value.

The success of this prefetching scheme in actually reducing cache misses is critically dependent on the amount of time available between the assignment of a value to a pointer and the first use of that value for an indirect memory access. That time interval has to be long enough for the corresponding block to be prefetched into the cache before an access is first made into the block. Depending on the system organization, the time to fetch a block into the cache may vary in the range of about 4 to 10 machine cycles, or about 4 to 10 RISC-style instructions. Of course, even if that time is not available between the assignment to a pointer and its first use, a gain still exists in the form of a shorter miss delay. To get an estimate of the above time interval, we counted the HLL statements in the critical loops in § 2.4 that are executed between loading a pointer and first indirecting through it †. The results were as follows:

≈ 50% of the cases (8 pointer loadings):   0 or 1 HLL statements
≈ 20% of the cases (3 pointer loadings):   2 or 3 HLL statements
≈ 30% of the cases (4 pointer loadings):   4 or more HLL statm.

This means that only in 30 to 50 % of the cases there is enough time for the prefetch to be complete before the first indirection through the pointer actually occurs.

It is possible for this time interval to be lengthened, and thus for the prefetching-hint scheme to yield better results, through a more *sophisticated programming technique*. In critical loops, the programmer can *preload* a local pointer with an address to be (potentially) used during the next loop iteration. For example:

/* Run through a list, doing some processing with its elements */

† These measurements are static; however, they were collected only from critical loops (§ 2.4).

```
struct node *current, *next;       /* local pointers */
next = head;
while ( (current=next) != NIL )
       { next = current→nxt;     /* preload */
       ...Do  the processing, using current→otherFields...
       }
```

In a few cases, a code rearrangement with similar effects could be made by an optimizing compiler. However, most cases are such that the prefetching will only be effective when done almost one whole loop iteration ahead of time. This usually requires the introduction of a new pointer variable by the programmer.

Even with this sophisticated programming technique, misses will still occur whenever a pointer to a structure is loaded with a value pointing into one cache block and is subsequently used to access a field of the corresponding structure which overflows onto the next cache block. This will happen most frequently with pointers pointing near the end of blocks or with structures that are larger than the block size. One solution can be to prefetch both the block pointed to by p and the next block whenever p is loaded with a value that points ''too close'' to a block's end. Another solution can be to try to allocate structures so that they do not cross cache block boundaries too often. Assuming a block size of 8 words = 32 bytes, this can be done trivially for structures of sizes 2, 4, or 8 words. In the static measurements reported in § 6.4.1 (B), the structure declarations that had exactly those sizes constituted 10%, 25%, and 10% of all structure declarations, respectively.

6.5   Multi-Port Memory Organization

Throughout this dissertation our focus has been the central processing unit of a von Neumann computer. The predominant pattern of simple operations applied to large volumes of operands was observed in typical examples of frequently occurring computations. As a consequence, priority was given to hardware support for fast operand accesses in the forms of multi-window register files, instruction fetch-and-sequence units, and data caches. However, the prevalent role of access to data or information is not confined to the interaction of the CPU with its surrounding fast storage devices. Also important is the access to bulk storage devices, to other processors, and to remote computing sites. This section concerns itself with the access to information in main memory. The use of memories with multiple ports will first be established. Then, a new device is proposed, a modified dynamic RAM chip, which effectively provides a second, independent, *sequential-access* port at a minor additional cost.

6.5.1 The Need for Multi-Port Memory Systems

Figure 6.5.1 presents an overview of various system organizations, showing their requirements for multi-port memory systems.

- (a) is a uni-processor, perhaps with a single cache memory. Slow I/O accesses (e.g. terminals, telephone lines) may be made via the CPU or via memory, but fast I/O accesses (e.g. disks, local-area-networks (LAN), raster displays) are always made by direct-memory-access (DMA) since their bandwidth is so high that the CPU cannot handle it. At least two high-bandwidth memory ports are seen to be needed: CPU and fast-I/O.

- (b) is a higher performance uni-processor with two memory-ports, one for instructions and one for data (§ 3.3.2, 3.3.3). This system may have separate instruction and data caches, as proposed in this chapter, but simultaneous misses in both caches are possible and require a memory port for each one of them. Such systems can be implemented with two separate main memory modules, one for instructions and one for data. However, it is also common to implement them with a single shared module, so that all available memory can be used regardless of whether there is little code and many data or vice versa.

- (c) is one possible multi-processor configuration. Here, the need for multiple memory ports is very high. Accessibility to the memory is, in fact, the limiting factor in system expandability.

- (d) is a possible organization of one node in a future multi-processor system. It consists of a uni-processor like (a) or (b), connected to other processors and I/O devices via a high-bandwidth network of interconnected communications components [Fuji83]. A separate supervisor CPU may

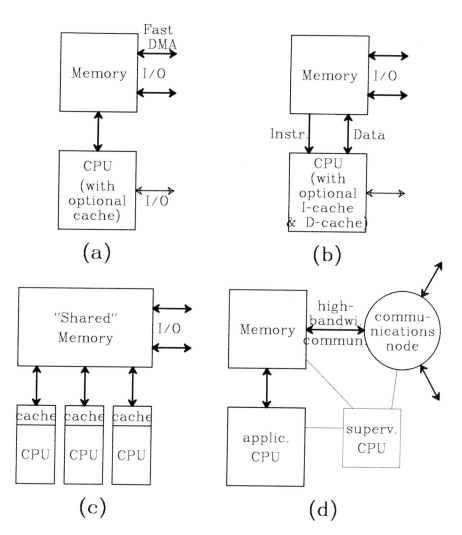

Figure 6.5.1: Need for Multi-Port Memories.

exist, to take care of communications overhead, paging, interrupt handling, etc. We consider this organization as more attractive than (c),
because it is expandable in a uniform manner.

Today, multi-port memories are made by providing time-shared access to a single physically available memory port. This is because true multi-port devices are prohibitively expensive for large storage systems, but also because most systems are of type (a) above with fast-I/O devices that have an average bandwidth that is still significantly lower than that of the CPU.

When multiple, asynchronous access requests are made to a single, shared memory port, contention will arise. Whenever simultaneous requests occur, all but one of the requesting devices will have to wait. For example, a RISC CPU uses the memory during all cycles; thus, it has to wait when an I/O access occurs. In a VAX-11/780 system, the processor is slowed by roughly 4% for each Mbyte/sec of average I/O traffic when its memory is 2-way interleaved, or by roughly 10% in the non-interleaved option [DEC81].

If the average bandwidth of the fast-I/O devices is significantly lower than that of the CPU -- and hence than that of the memory -- then memory contention will only have a minor negative effect on CPU performance. The following table gives a feeling of the bandwidth requirements of the various devices that may be connected to a memory system in organizations like the ones in fig. 6.5.1. Since real values vary widely, the table only gives some typical examples.

Example of Memory Access Characteristics by Various Devices.			
Device	Size of access (Bytes)	Average Bandwidth (MBytes/s)	Peak Bandwidth (Mbytes/s)
CPU	4	10.	12.
Cache	32	4.	20.
Slow I/O (Terminal,etc)	1	0.0001	0.001
Fast I/O (Disk, LAN)	2000	0.3	1.

Thus, in typical systems of today, the average bandwidth of their few fast-I/O devices represents only about one tenth of the CPU bandwidth. This is a tolerable load which does not degrade CPU performance too much, when the CPU and I/O share a single memory port with a cycle-time approximately equal to the CPU cycle-time.

This situation, however, will probably change in the future. In our view, systems will evolve towards organization (d), since expandable multi-processors will be desirable and feasible. The communications bandwidth will increase, both because of advances in technology, and because of the need for more closely-coupled parallel execution. This bandwidth increase will place a heavy load on the memory system. It is important to notice, however, that, whereas the CPU performs random accesses to the memory, a fast I/O device or a communications network performs *serial* accesses most of the time, since large pieces of consecutive memory (e.g. pages) are copied in or out of the memory. The internal organization of dynamic RAM chips is such that it allows the inexpensive addition of a second *serial-access* port to them, thus solving the CPU-I/O contention problem.

6.5.2 DRAM Chips With Secondary Serial-Access Port

The top part of figure 6.5.2 shows a typical internal organization of a dynamic RAM chip. Every time an access is made, the whole row along the activated word-line is read out of the storage array into the sense amplifiers. Then, a single bit is selected by the column address. Thus, there is a huge difference of about 3 orders of magnitude in the bandwidth of on-chip and off-chip reading operations. In a memory system, the chips' row-address is typically the physical page number. Thus, on every access, one whole memory page is read into the sense amplifiers of the memory chips. For example, if a 1 Mbyte memory consists of 32 256-Kbit chips like the one shown in fig. 6.5.2, then, on every memory access, 32 rows of 1-Kbit each are read in all the chips, amounting to a total of a 32-Kbit or a 4-Kbyte page.

Even though a whole page may be read inside the DRAM chips, only a single word is selected out of it and transmitted off-chip. Many recent DRAM chips offer a *nibble* or *page* mode of access. Under the former mode, four adjacent bits (words) out of the row (page) are serially transmitted off-chip, with a very short delay between subsequent bits. Under the latter mode, any subsequent access to the same row (page) can be made with a shorter delay than the first one, by just supplying a new column-address to the chips. These modes of access make some of the high on-chip bandwidth available to off-chip accesses. They can be used to speed up cache-block accesses and sequential I/O as long as it is uninterrupted by references to other pages. The applicability of these modes to

CPU accesses is limited because the CPU does not usually ask for adjacent words
or for words from the same page on consecutive memory transactions.

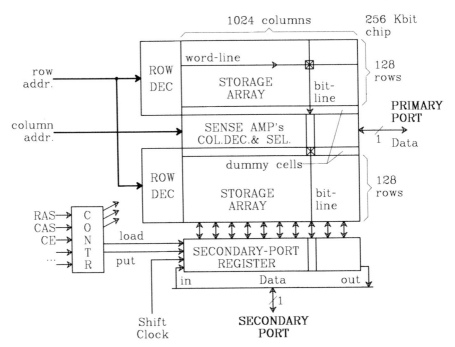

Figure 6.5.2: DRAM Chip with Secondary Serial Port.

The lower part of figure 6.5.2, shows the proposed addition to a conventional DRAM chip. It consists of a shift-register of size equal to one row. It has
parallel connections to the bit lines of the storage array and a serial connection to
one pin of the chip. One additional chip pin is used as its *independent* shift
clock. This proposed "secondary-port register" can be loaded in one memory
cycle with the contents of the row which is being read during that cycle. On the
scale of the entire memory system, this corresponds to coping an entire page into
the secondary-port registers of the memory chips. Once this page transfer has
been done, the parallel connections between the secondary-port registers and the
bit-lines may be disabled, and their serial off-chip ports may be enabled. These

now provide a second *totally independent, serial-access* memory port, which even has its own (asynchronous) clock. Through this "secondary serial-access port", the entire page can be transferred to the I/O device at the latter's own rate of transfer. This rate can be higher than the primary-port rate, because the shift-register is faster than the dynamic storage array. Of course, the inverse of the above scenario can be followed for transfers from the I/O device to the secondary-port register and finally into an arbitrary memory page.

The cost of this secondary memory-chip port is roughly similar to that of the sense-amplifiers in terms of silicon area: about 1/10th of the chip. In terms of pins, 3 additional ones are needed -- one for the serial data, one for the serial clock, and one for controlling the mode of page transfer †. A hidden cost of this system arises from the fact that it requires the page-number to be the *row-address* instead of the column-address. The row-address is required to be available to the chip at the very beginning of the memory access. Thus, virtual-to-physical address translation cannot be performed in parallel with row decoding and bit-line sensing, as it is possible when the page-number is used as column address.

In conclusion, the proposed secondary serial-access memory port will be advantageous for memories in systems with high I/O bandwidth, such that the CPU-I/O contention for memory cycles results in a heavier penalty than the address translation delay that the new memory organization may incur. In general, small additions or reorganizations of hardware may lead to changes in system architecture that can result in large gains in performance. In all cases, it is important to first identify the actual bottleneck areas so that the added hardware can be as effective as possible.

---

† one additional serial data pin is required if simultaneous, synchronous input *and* output into/from the secondary-port register is desired.

Chapter 7

Conclusions

Single-chip implementation of a general-purpose von Neumann processor offers advantages of low cost and of high performance owing to the high bandwidth of on-chip communications. However, even in Very Large Scale Integrated (VLSI) circuits, the limited transistors that are available on a single chip constitute a scarce resource when used to implement such a CPU. In this dissertation, the efficient use of these silicon resources was studied, showing that a Reduced Instruction Set Computer (RISC) architecture is advantageous, because it allows the integration of units providing fast access to operands and instructions, while still supporting the high-performance execution of the simple operations required during most part of general-purpose computations.

In chapter 2, the nature of general-purpose von Neumann computations was studied. Even programs that are heavily oriented to numerical floating-point computations execute an equally high number of array references, simple index arithmetic, and loop control instructions. In non-numerical programs, floating-point computations are replaced by copying or compare-and-branch instructions, and array references are often replaced by indirect accesses through pointers. This shows the crucial importance of fast operand accessing, simple address arithmetic, and fast compare-and-branch execution. The high percentage of references to local scalar variables ($\approx$ 60 % of all variable references) and the fact that most procedures have few such variables (a dozen or less) makes hardware support for fast operand accessing mandatory. The narrow range ($\approx$ $\pm$3) of dynamic procedure nesting depth fluctuations for extended periods of time, makes a small set of overlapping register windows a viable approach.

The above findings led to the formulation of the Reduced Instruction Set Computer (RISC) concept and to the definition of the Berkeley RISC architecture, which became the basis of a large group project. Within this project, a second NMOS implementation of the Berkeley RISC processor, called RISC II, was designed, laid-out, debugged, and successfully tested after fabrication, in collaboration with Robert Sherburne.

The Berkeley RISC architecture, as described in chapter 3, is register-to-register oriented. It has simple instructions, a simple and orthogonal instruction-format, and a regular timing model that fits all instructions. Fast operand accesses are supported by a large register-file with multiple overlapping windows, where scalar arguments and local variables of procedures are allocated by default until the window is filled. Pipelining is utilized to keep the operational units busy executing the primitive operations selected by the compiler and optimizer. The combined effect of the 138 registers, organized in 8 windows, and of the 3-stage pipeline yields a machine of significantly higher performance than other commercial processors built in comparable technologies but with complex instructions and non-optimal use of registers. The size of programs compiled for RISC is not much larger than it is when compiled for other architectures, even though only simple instructions with a simple but code-inefficient format are available to the compiler.

The change away from the traditional trend towards instruction sets of increasing complexity resulted in a radical change in the allocation of the chip area to the various CPU functions. As shown in chapter 4, the control section of RISC II occupies only 10% of the area, in contrast with other processors with complex instruction sets, where the control and micro-program ROM occupy more than half the chip area. Scarce silicon resources are thus freed and used more effectively for the implementation of the large register file. The simplicity of the processor significantly contributes to its speed by reducing the number of gate-delays in the critical path and also by reducing the physical size, and thus the parasitic capacitances, of the circuit elements. Designing, laying-out, and debugging the simple RISC II processor required about five times less human effort than what is usual for other microprocessors. Chips were functionally correct and ran at the predicted speed on first silicon due to careful simulation and modeling, as described in chapter 5.

Future VLSI technology will allow the integration of larger systems on a single chip. Beyond multi-window register-files, such technologies will also allow on-chip support for fast access to other important elements of computations: instructions, and non-scalar operands. Chapter 6 proposed suitable organizations for such units. Remote-PC instruction-fetch-&-sequence units keep the program-counter and its associated logic close to the place where it is being used and provide reduced communication costs and more parallelism in executing jumps. When combined with a dual-port instruction-cache, they allow single-cycle compare-&-branch instructions and transparent unconditional branches, both of which are frequent instructions in general-purpose computations (about 1 out of 4 instructions). Instruction-caches also allow the CPU to effectively see two independent memory ports and make it possible to access data in memory while the next instruction is being fetched. Further inclusion of a data-cache allows address-computation to partially overlap data access, thus making possible single-cycle data-memory-access instructions.

For the foreseeable future, Reduced Instruction Set Computer Architectures appear to be the most effective way to use the scarce chip resources to support the crucial need of general-purpose computations for fast access to operands and instructions.

Appendix A

Detailed Description
of the RISC II Architecture

This appendix describes in detail the architecture of the RISC II CPU NMOS chip. It is a complement to chapter 3.

Some of the minor details of the RISC II architecture are ''by-products'' of its implementation. Most of these are points that were left unspecified in the original architecture. One important exception was mentioned in § 3.1.2. Register-indexed store instructions can only have an immediate source-2 -- not a register R_{s2} (fig. A.4.4). This restriction was imposed for implementation reasons. For similar reasons, this chip does not implement the pointer-to-register scheme (§ 3.2.3). On the other hand, it has some additional features: (1) conditional returns, and (2) compatibility with Expanding Instruction Caches [Patt83].

In this appendix the RISC II architecture is described from various points of view:

- definition of the user-visible CPU state (§ A.1);
- description of the CPU interface to the outside world (memory, I/O, interrupts) (§ A.2);
- discussion of the way in which instructions are sequenced (§ A.3);
- description of the instruction set, the instruction format, and the effect that the execution of each instruction has on the user-visible state of the CPU

and on the CPU interface to the outside world (§ A.4);

- specification of the actions taken on interrupts/traps (§ A.5).

A.1   User-Visible State of the CPU

The User-Visible State (u-v state) of the CPU is the state of the processor chip
that remains after execution of an instruction has completed, and before execution of the next instruction begins. The "future" of the processor depends, at
that point, only on that state. The above "point in time", may not be well
defined in the implementation, because of pipelining. However, the RISC architecture precisely defines the *state* of the CPU at that point, since it considers
instruction execution to be indivisible and entirely sequential. The implementation must guarantee that the overall result of executing an arbitrary program on
the real hardware will be the same as predicted by the architecture for purely
sequential execution of the same program.

Here, we must draw a distinction between the "normal user" and the
"interrupt-handler programmer" (i-h programmer) †. The "normal user" does
not see the interrupts; what (s)he considers *one* instruction may in fact be an
instruction that was aborted and then restarted after an interrupt handler completed its task. Such a user has his/her u-v state. The "interrupt-handler programmer" has a *finer-grain definition* of what an instruction is; for him/her interrupts and aborted instructions are clearly visible. Thus, (s)he needs to have additional visible state for the interrupt-handler to work with, while the normal user's
visible state is left unaltered.

Figure A.1.1 shows the RISC II User-Visible State. The register file has
138 32-bit registers, accessible by an addressing pair: (WindowNumber .
RegisterNumber). The WindowNumber ranges from 0 to 7 and is *always* provided by CWP=PSW<12:10>. The RegisterNumber is provided by the individual
instruction accessing the register; it ranges from 31 to 0, with 31 to 26 overlapping with the parent (caller), 25 to 16 being the locals, 15 to 10 overlapping with

---

† In this section the word interrupt is used to signify both interrupts and traps.

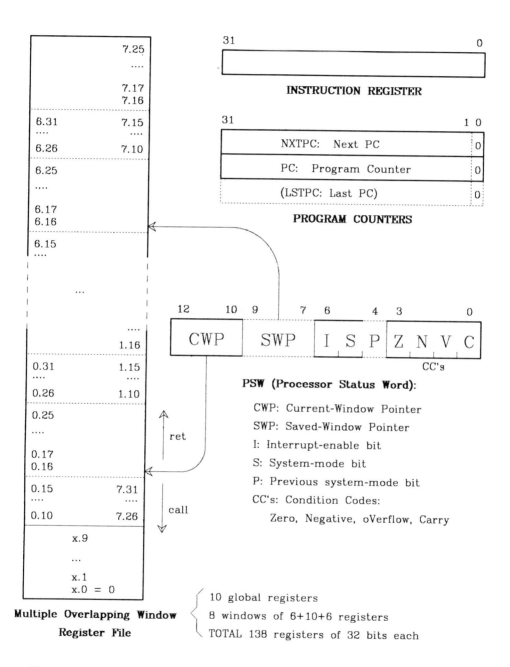

Figure A.1.1: User-Visible State of RISC II CPU.

the child (callee), and 9 to 0 being the globals. Register-0 always has the (hard-wired) value 0; writing into it is allowed, but has no effect whatsoever.

The PSW has 13 bits containing various information. The CWP specifies the current window, and SWP is the limit-value for detecting register-file over/under-flows. The fact that they are shown to point to register-16 has no particular significance for the RISC II CPU; this is in analogy to the pointer-to-register scheme (§ 3.2.3). The I bit enables/disables interrupts. The S bit shows the current CPU privileges. The P bit is a place to save the previous value of the S bit when the latter is altered (set) on interrupts. The four remaining bits of PSW are the condition codes.

The SWP and the P bit are parts of the state visible by the i-h programmer only. Since register-file over/underflows are taken care of by an interrupt-handler, the "normal user" is given the illusion of a register-file with infinitely many windows ‡. The i-h programmer uses the SWP to detect over/underflows of the *real* register-file, the necessary window save/restore operations are carried out, and subsequently the value of the SWP is changed to reflect that fact. If the normal user reads SWP, (s)he may find "random values" in it (i.e. values that do not depend on his/her program alone). Similarly, the P bit is used to save a part of the normal-user-visible state before that latter is altered on an instruction abortion, so that it can be restored later; the normal user is given the illusion of an uninterrupted instruction execution.

The definition of the remaining four words of u-v state is more difficult and does not completely correspond to the implementation. The reason is that their values are of a *dynamic* nature. They are implicitly and automatically changed by the execution of *every* instruction; and thus cannot be *preserved* and read by some other instruction at a later time. However, they do belong to the u-v state, since they depend on the previous instruction(s), and they determine the future activities of the processor.

At the (conceptual) moment when an instruction completes execution and the next one has not yet started executing, the Instruction Register contains the instruction to be executed next. The PC contains the address of that next-to-be-

---

‡ If we wanted to be very precise, we should have shown that in fig. A.1.1, together with a CWP whose existence, but not its value, is known to the normal user.

executed instruction. This information would in general be redundant since the instruction is already known, but it is needed for PC-relative addressing.

At the end of an instruction the u-v state contains the address of the next instruction and also the instruction itself. This is a consequence of the delayed-branch scheme, which makes the instruction-fetch/execute pipeline visible to the user (§ 3.1.3). This also explains the existence of NXTPC in the u-v state. NXTPC is the address of the instruction to be executed subsequently after the one contained in the Instruction Register. It plays the role of PC in other computers. NXTPC is determined by the instruction that just finished executing, and not by the instruction that will execute next, in accordance with the delayed-jump scheme. The LSTPC register is part of the i-h programmer visible state only. It contains the address of the instruction which just finished executing. Its purpose is to hold the value of the PC when an instruction is aborted due to an interrupt. The PC, in turn, holds the value of the NXTPC, while NXTPC is used for fetching the first instruction of the interrupt-handler. The three PC's always have a 0 least significant bit, since RISC II instructions are always half-word aligned in main-memory.

The u-v state remains unaltered during the "first part" of the execution cycle, when the processor reads some parts of it in order to compute some new values to be written back into the state during the "last part" of the execution cycle. In particular, PC-relative instructions will use the value that the PC has at the beginning of the execution cycle.

A.2   Interface between CPU and Outside World

The RISC II CPU communicates with the outside world by read and write accesses from/into a 4Gbyte virtual address-space. Thus, all I/O and System-Control functions are memory-mapped. Figure A.2.1 shows the signals that come in and out of the CPU.

For each memory access, the CPU issues an address and specifies the access type by the Read/Write signal. It also issues some additional information, which the peripheral devices may or may not use: (i) whether the processor is currently

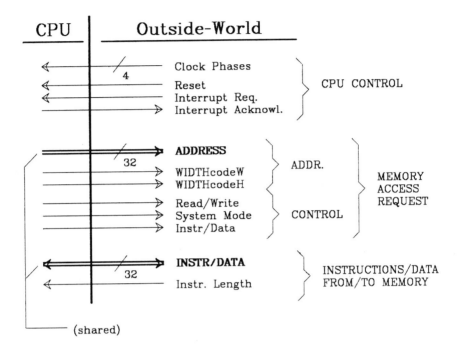

Figure A.2.1: CPU - Outside World Interface.

in user or system mode, and (ii) whether the CPU interprets the accessed item as instruction or as data (this signal is always "data" for write accesses). Addresses are virtual, 32 bit wide, and refer to bytes in memory.

The RISC II architecture understands and supports byte data (8 bit wide), half-word data (16 bit wide), and word data (32 bit wide). Figure A.2.2(a) shows the possible alignments that those types may have in memory and the address used to refer to each one of them (addresses shown are in decimal). Every item must be aligned so that, if the whole memory were packed with items of the same width and the same alignment, no item would cross word boundaries. The address of an item is the address of the least-significant byte in it, with addresses increasing towards more-significant bytes.

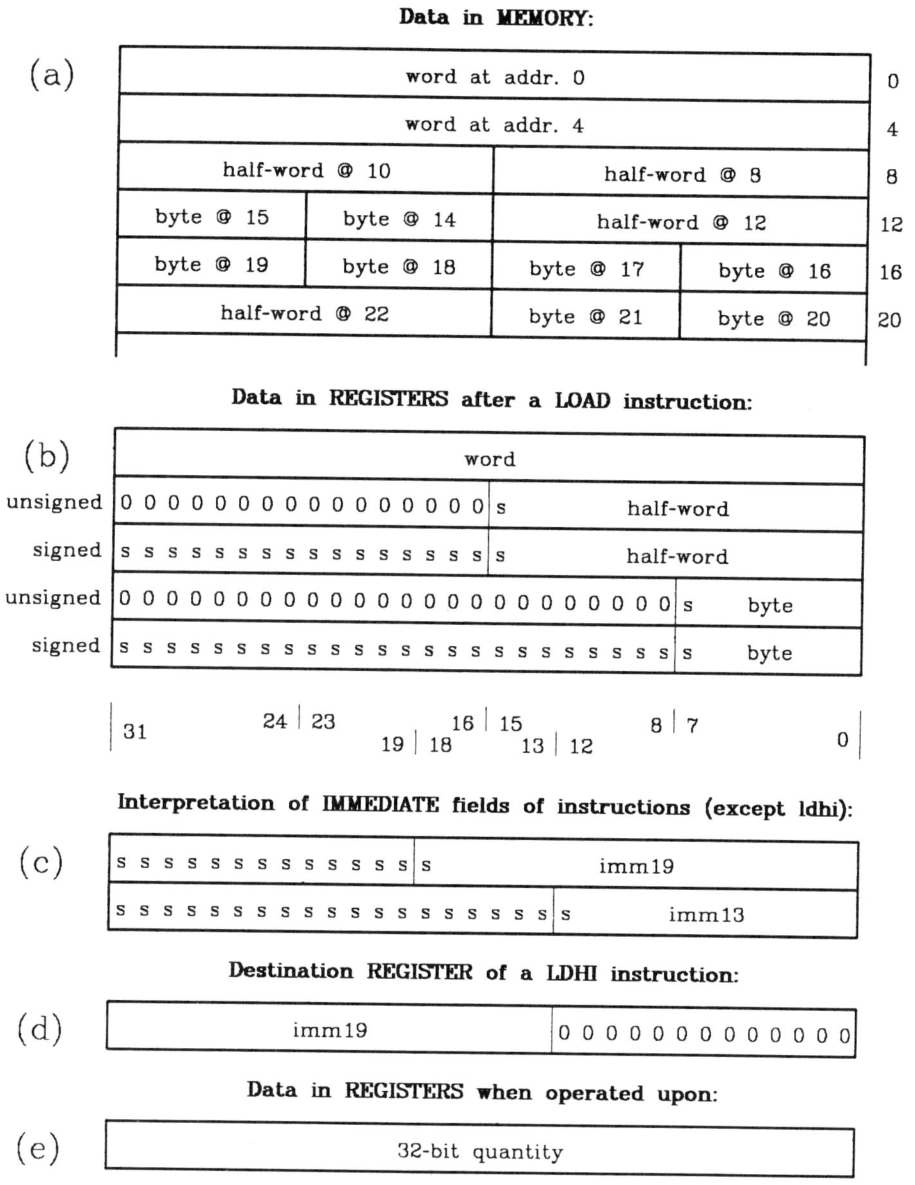

Data in MEMORY:

(a)

word at addr. 0		0
word at addr. 4		4
half-word @ 10	half-word @ 8	8
byte @ 15 / byte @ 14	half-word @ 12	12
byte @ 19 / byte @ 18	byte @ 17 / byte @ 16	16
half-word @ 22	byte @ 21 / byte @ 20	20

Data in REGISTERS after a LOAD instruction:

(b)

	word	
unsigned	0 0 0 0 0 0 0 0 0 0 0 0 0 0 0 0 s	half-word
signed	s s s s s s s s s s s s s s s s s	half-word
unsigned	0 0 0 0 0 0 0 0 0 0 0 0 0 0 0 0 0 0 0 0 0 0 0 0 s	byte
signed	s s s s s s s s s s s s s s s s s s s s s s s s s	byte

```
 |31          24|23                16|15         8|7          0|
                      19|18       13|12
```

Interpretation of IMMEDIATE fields of instructions (except ldhi):

(c)

s s s s s s s s s s s s s	imm19
s s s s s s s s s s s s s s s s s s s	imm13

Destination REGISTER of a LDHI instruction:

(d)

imm19	0 0 0 0 0 0 0 0 0 0 0 0 0

Data in REGISTERS when operated upon:

(e)

32-bit quantity

Figure A.2.2:   Width, Addresses, and Alignment.

The memory of a RISC II system is organized in words, having, however, separate write-enable controls for the four byte-wide fields (byte-banks) in it, so that it can selectively write some but not all of the bytes in a word. Read accesses always read a whole word. The two least-significant address bits are discarded (considered to be zero) and the corresponding word is read and given to the CPU. Further selection and alignment of narrower data items is performed inside the CPU. For write accesses, the CPU always outputs a full 32-bit word onto the bus. However, only *some* of the bytes in that word are to be written into the corresponding bytes of the addressed word. Figure A.2.3 shows an example. The target word is determined as before by considering the 2 LS-bits of the address to be zero. The particular bytes to be written are determined by the two original least-significant address bits, and by the "width-code bits" (fig. A.2.1), according to the table in figure A.2.3. The width-code bits indicate the type of item to be written. They could be encoded in one bit, but the RISC II chip leaves them unencoded. Bit<i> of the target memory word is written with bit<i>of the word output on the bus (if the corresponding byte-bank is enabled); in other words, the memory does not need to perform any alignment.

Instruction fetches need not be different from data reads in a simple RISC II system. All instructions that the RISC II CPU understands are 32-bit wide. In fact, the RISC II CPU chip uses the same bus and timing for instruction and data fetches. However, the RISC II CPU is also compatible with Expanding Instruction Caches [Patt83]. These are instruction caches that receive from memory both 16- and 32-bit wide instructions. They "expand" the 16-bit ones into equivalent 32-bit instructions, which they subsequently supply to the CPU. All this is transparent for the CPU, which only sees 32-bit instructions, except for the fact that NXTPC has to follow the real memory address of the instructions, i.e. it has to get incremented by 2 or by 4, according to the length of the lastly fetched instruction. This is the purpose of the instruction-length signal going into the CPU (fig. A.2.1). In the absence of an expanding cache, this signal must be permanently set to "4 bytes". In the presence of such a cache, it is the cache who provides it.

Finally, the "outside world" has some control over the CPU by means of the clock phases and the reset- and interrupt-request signals. By means of the clock phases, the CPU can be slowed down, or even stopped temporarily, which is useful for example, during the handling of a cache miss. A single interrupt

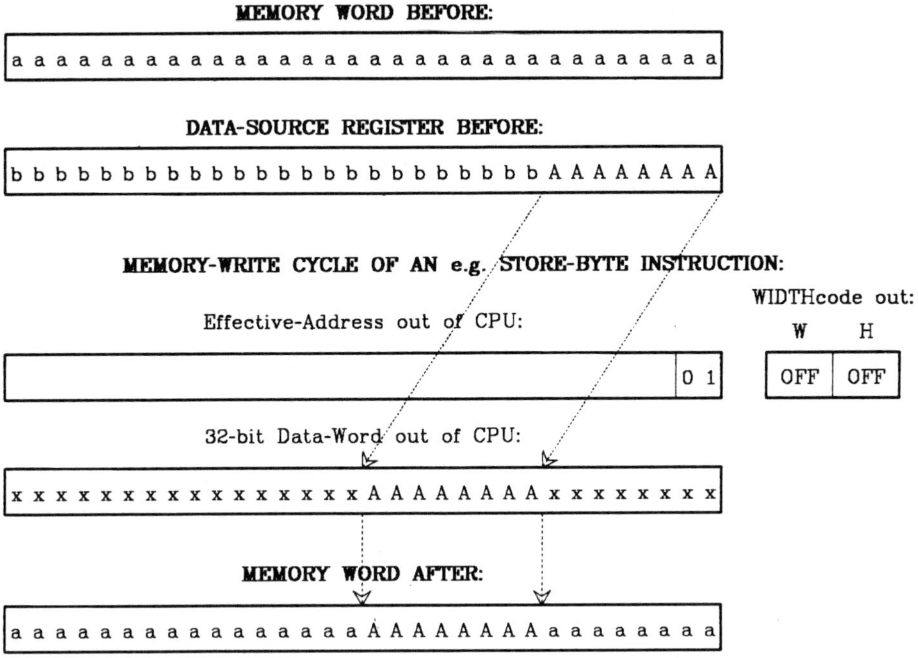

Figure A.2.3: Storing Data of various Widths.

INSTR	INFORMATION THAT THE CPU OUTPUTS			MEMORY-BYTE-BANKS THAT SHOULD BE OVERWRITTEN			
	WIDTHcodeW	WIDTHcodeH	eff_addr<1:0>	<31:24>	<23:16>	<15:8>	<7:0>
stw	ON	OFF	00	W	W	W	W
sth	OFF	ON	00			W	W
			10	W	W		
stb	OFF	OFF	00				W
			01			W	
			10		W		
			11	W			

request signal is provided. It is assumed that interrupt prioritizing is done outside the CPU. The reset signal acts as a non-maskable interrupt.

A.3   Instruction Execution Sequencing

RISC II sequences instruction execution in the usual von Neumann way, except for the visibility of the fetch/execute overlap which results in the delayed jump scheme (§ 3.1.3), and for the compatibility with Expanding Instruction-Caches (§ A.2). Figure A.4.5 describes control-transfer instructions.

The instruction-fetch process operates in parallel with the instruction-execute process and relatively independently from it. Out of the user-visible state, the fetch process uses the PC's, and the execute process uses the register file and PSW. The two processes communicate via the instruction register in the "forward direction" and via the control-transfer instructions in the "backwards direction". When an interrupt (or trap) occurs, progress of the execute process is aborted, and that process is inhibited from altering its u-v state. However, the fetch process is allowed to proceed, after an alteration is made to it so that it starts fetching instructions from the interrupt handler routine. These points will be discussed further in § A.5.

A.4   Instruction Set

Figure A.4.1 shows the two instruction formats of the RISC II CPU. Figure A.4.2 shows the binary and symbolic opcodes of the 39 RISC II instructions. The opcode uniquely determines whether the instruction has the short-immediate or the long-immediate format, and figure A.4.2 shows that correspondence. The opcode also uniquely determines the interpretation of the DEST field of the instruction (fig. A.4.1(a)), and fig. A.4.2 shows that correspondence as well. The format of the shortSOURCE2 field of the short-immediate instructions is determined by *its* leading bit, and not by the opcode (fig. A.4.1(b)). Figure

1. SHORT-IMMEDIATE FORMAT:

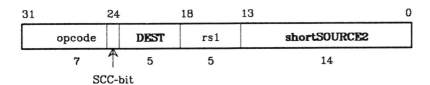

2. LONG-IMMEDIATE FORMAT:

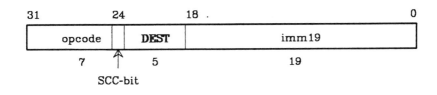

INSTRUCTION-FIELD FORMATS:

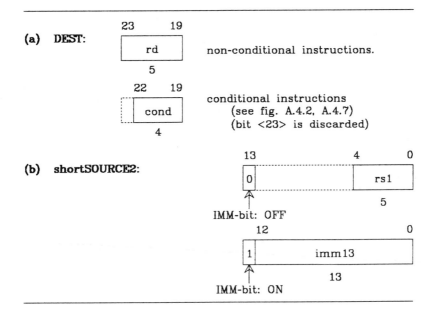

Figure A.4.1:   RISC II Instruction Format.

	000xxxx	001xxxx	010xxxx	011xxxx	1xxxxxx			
xxx0000								
xxx0001	**calli**	sll						
xxx0010	getpsw	sra						
xxx0011	**getlpc**	srl						
xxx0100	**putpsw**	ldhi						
xxx0101		and						
xxx0110		or	ldxw	stxw				
xxx0111		xor	ldrw	strw				
xxx1000	callx	add	ldxhu					
xxx1001	callr	addc	ldrhu					
xxx1010			ldxhs	stxh				
xxx1011			ldrhs	strh				
xxx1100	Ⓒ jmpx	sub	ldxbu					
xxx1101	Ⓒ jmpr	subc	ldrbu					
xxx1110	Ⓒ ret	subi	ldxbs	stxb				
xxx1111	Ⓒ **reti**	subci	ldrbs	strb				

Ⓒ : conditional instructions: DEST-field is cond (see fig. A.4.1(a)).

 double boxes : long-immediate format instructions (fig. A.4.1(2)).

empty boxes: illegal opcodes.

calli, getlpc, putpsw, reti: privileged instructions.

Figure A.4.2: The RISC II opcodes.

A.4.2 also shows which instructions are privileged. An attempt to execute a privileged instruction while the System-mode bit is OFF causes an immediate trap which prevents the instruction from executing (§ A.5). A trap is also caused if execution of an illegal instruction (one with unassigned opcode) is attempted (notice that all opcodes with a leading bit equal to 1 are unassigned). RISC II has the same 39 instructions as RISC I, but it has different opcodes.

The instruction set can be subdivided into five groups of instructions, which are described in figures A.4.3 through A.4.8 and discussed in the next paragraphs.

Register-to-register OP instructions: Figure A.4.3 shows all the instructions of the second column of fig. A.4.2, except for *ldhi*. They include shift, logical, and integer-arithmetic operations. They all have the short-immediate format. They operate on register rs1 of the current window and on the source-2. Source-2 may be register rs2 of the current window or the immediate constant imm13 contained in the instruction. Registers are always interpreted as 32-bit quantities (fig. A.2.2(e)), and imm13 is always sign-extended (fig. A.2.2(c)). The result is written into register rd of the current window, and the instruction may additionally update the Condition Codes. Remember that register-0 always has the value 0 and that writing into it has no effect.

Load instructions: Figure A.4.4 shows all the instructions of the third column of figure A.4.2. They perform read accesses from the virtual address space. The effective address for the access is the sum of rs1 and shortSOURCE2 for register-indexed loads (which have the letter x in their symbolic opcodes), or the sum of PC and imm19 for PC-relative loads (which have the letter r in their symbolic opcodes). There are separate load instructions for words (w), half-words (h), and bytes(b). For the two latter cases, there are instructions for loading those quantities as signed (s) or unsigned (u) numbers. The addressed word is first read from memory, as discussed in § A.2. Then, the desired part of the word is extracted from it, right-aligned, sign-extended or zero-filled, and written into rd. (The "desired part" of the word is defined by the instruction and by the two least-significant bits of the effective address; see fig. A.2.2(b).) The CC's may optionally be updated according to the value placed into rd.

Store instructions: Figure A.4.4 also shows all the instructions of the fourth column of figure A.4.2. They perform write accesses into the virtual address space. The effective address for the access is computed in a fashion similar to

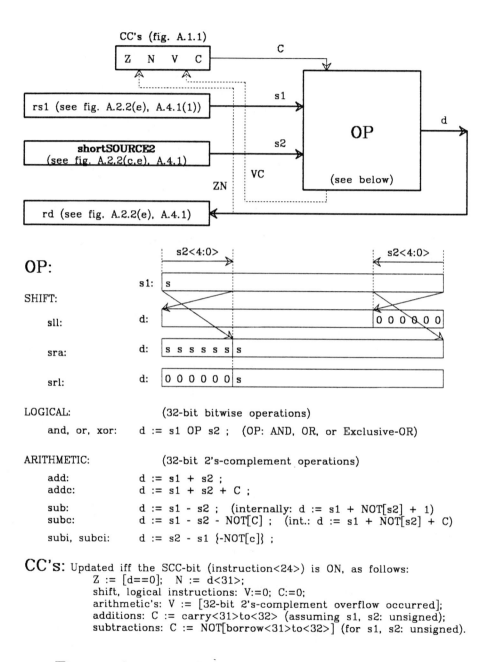

CC's: Updated iff the SCC-bit (instruction<24>) is ON, as follows:
        Z := [d==0];   N := d<31>;
        shift, logical instructions: V:=0; C:=0;
        arithmetic's: V := [32-bit 2's-complement overflow occurred];
        additions: C := carry<31>to<32> (assuming s1, s2: unsigned);
        subtractions: C := NOT[borrow<31>to<32>] (for s1, s2: unsigned).

Figure A.4.3:   ALU and Shift Instructions.

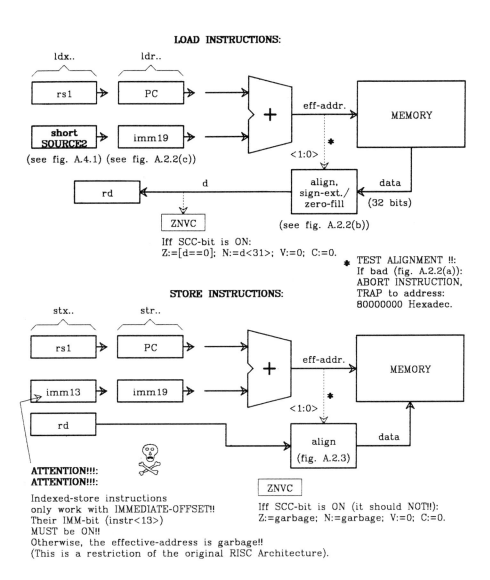

Figure A.4.4:   Load   and   Store   Instructions.

that for loads, except that for register-indexed addressing, shortSOURCE2 *must* be an immediate (§ 3.1.2). The CPU properly aligns the item to be stored, according to its width specifyed by the instruction type and to the 2 LS-bits of the effective address (fig. A.2.3). It also outputs information about the item's width, so that the memory selectively writes only some of the four byte-banks (§ A.2).

Control-Transfer Instructions: Figures A.4.5 through A.4.7 describe the jump, subroutine call, and return instructions. Figures A.4.5 through A.4.7 describe them. The (conditional) jump and (unconditional) call instructions compute their effective target address like the load instructions do (register-indexed or PC-relative). Only a register-indexed version of the return instruction is provided, because that's all that is needed. There is a return-from-interrupt instruction which will be discussed in § A.5. Return instructions are conditional. Figure A.4.6 contains the details of the window manipulation for call and return instructions (§ 3.2.2). Attention is drawn to the fact that the call instructions read their source register(s) from the old window, whereas they write their destination into the new one. Figure A.4.7 shows the branch conditions employed by conditional-transfer instructions.

Miscellaneous instructions: These are shown in figure A.4.8. The *ldhi* instruction is used for loading the most-significant part of long immediate constants into registers (fig. A.2.2(d)). The *getlpc* instruction is used as the first instruction of every interrupt-handler routine in order to save LSTPC into rd (see § A.5). The *getpsw* and *putpsw* instructions are used for manipulating the PSW in an arbitrary fashion, including saving it before interrupts nest, and restoring it at a later time. The *calli* instruction is used by the hardware interrupt mechanism. The *getlpc* and the *calli* read a part of the i-h programmer visible state, and their effect is therefore not transparent to interrupts. *Calli* is intended to be used only by the hardware interrupt mechanism, and *getlpc* should be used only as the first instruction of an interrupt handling routine (§ A.5) or at a place where interrupts are disabled. If these two instructions are executed in a different context, with interrupts enabled, their result depends on whether they themselves are interrupted or not. If they are not interrupted, they will yield the address of their previous instruction. If they are interrupted, they will yield the address of the last instruction of the interrupt-handler which serviced the interrupt.

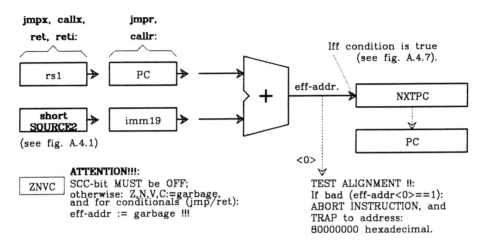

jmpx, callx,   **jmpr,**
ret, reti: **callr:**

rs1 ➤   PC ➤

short
SOURCE2 ➤   imm19 ➤
(see fig. A.4.1)

Iff condition is true
(see fig. A.4.7).

eff-addr.   NXTPC

PC

ZNVC

ATTENTION!!!:
SCC-bit MUST be OFF;
otherwise: Z,N,V,C:=garbage,
and for conditionals (jmp/ret):
eff-addr := garbage !!!

<0>

TEST ALIGNMENT !!:
If bad (eff-addr<0>==1):
ABORT INSTRUCTION, and
TRAP to address:
80000000 hexadecimal.

DELAYED JUMP SCHEME:
(Result of Fetch/Execute Overlap)

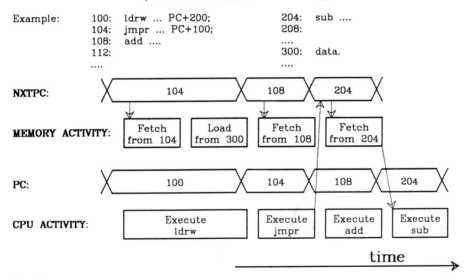

Example: 100: ldrw ... PC+200;   204: sub ....
            104: jmpr ... PC+100;   208:
            108: add ....
            112:                            300: data.
            ....

NXTPC: 104   108   204

MEMORY ACTIVITY: Fetch   Load   Fetch   Fetch
                   from 104 from 300 from 108 from 204

PC: 100   104   108   204

CPU ACTIVITY: Execute   Execute Execute Execute
                   ldrw   jmpr   add   sub

time ➙

Figure A.4.5:   Control Transfer - Delayed Jumps.

Figure A.4.6:   Control-Transfer Instructions.

Instructions:	Effect & Notes:
jmpx, jmpr:	Iff condition is true (see fig.A.4.7), then control is transferred, as shown in fig. A.4.5.
callx, callr:	(1) Transfer Control (see fig. A.4.5); (2) CWP := CWP-1 modulo 8 (change window - fig. A.1.1). (3) rd := PC (save PC into destination-register); **NOTES:** (a) the rs1 (& rs2) register(s) specified in the instruction, are read from the OLD window; (b) the PC value that is saved is the PC of the call instruction itself; (c) the PC is saved into register number rd of the NEW window; (d) if the change of CWP would result in a new value that would be equal to SWP (fig. A.1.1), then the call instruction is ABORTED, and the processor TRAPS to address 80000020 Hexadec. (if PSW_I is ON) (Reg-File Overflow occurred).
ret:	Iff condition is true (see fig. A.4.7), then: (1) Transfer Control (see fig. A.4.5); (2) CWP := CWP+1 modulo 8 (change window - fig. A.1.1). **NOTES:** (a) the rs1 (& rs2) register(s) specified in the instruction, are read from the OLD window; (b) the normal use of this instruction is with target addr. rs1+8 (with rs1=rd of the call). (c) if the condition is true, and if the change of CWP would result in a new value that would be equal to SWP (fig. A.1.1), then the return instr. is ABORTED, and the processor TRAPS to address 80000030 Hexadec. (if PSW_I is ON) (Reg-File Underflow occurred).
reti:	Iff condition is true (see fig. A.4.7), then: (1) Transfer Control (see fig. A.4.5); (2) CWP := CWP+1 modulo 8 (change window - fig. A.1.1). (3) Modify PSW: I:=ON (enable interrupts); S:=P . **NOTES:** Same as for ret.

Figure A.4.7: The RISC II Jump Conditions.

CODE	SYMBOL	NAME	MEANING
0001	gt	greater than (cmp signed)	$\overline{(N \oplus V) + Z}$
0010	le	less or equal (cmp signed)	$(N \oplus V) + Z$
0011	ge	greater or equal (cmp sign.)	$\overline{N \oplus V}$
0100	lt	less than (cmp signed)	$N \oplus V$
0101	hi	higher than (cmp unsigned)	$\overline{C + Z}$
0110	los	lower or same (cmp unsign.)	$\overline{C} + Z$
0111	lo / nc	lower than (cmp unsigned) / no carry	$\overline{C}$
1000	his / c	higher or same (cmp uns.) / carry	C
1001	pl	plus (tst signed)	$\overline{N}$
1010	mi	minus (tst signed)	N
1011	ne	not equal	$\overline{Z}$
1100	eq	equal	Z
1101	nv	no overflow (signed arithm.)	$\overline{V}$
1110	v	overflow (signed arithmetic)	V
1111	alw	always	1

CODE: This is the "cond"-field (instruction<22:19>) (see fig. A.4.1(a)).
SYMBOL: This is how the condition is represented in Assembly.
MEANING: The condition is true if and only if the value of this function of PSW<3:0> is 1.
$\oplus$: Exclusive-OR.

Figure A.4.8: Miscellaneous Instructions.

Instr.:	Effect & Notes:
ldhi:	(1) rd := imm19 << 13 -- see figure A.2.2(d); (2) Iff SCC-bit (instr.<24>) is ON, then: Z := [dest==0] ; N := dest<31> ; V,C := 0.
getlpc:	(1) rd := LSTPC (fig. A.1.1); (2) Iff SCC-bit (instr.<24>) is ON, then: Z := [LSTPC==0] ; N := LSTPC<31> ; V,C := garbage. **NOTES:** (a) the rs1, shortSOURCE2 fields are discarded; (b) the value of LSTPC, which is saved in rd, is equal to the value that the PC had during the execution of the previous instruction. (c) this instr. is NOT transparent to interrupts.
getpsw:	(1) rd := (-1)<31:13> concatenated PSW<12:0> ; Iff SCC-bit is ON, (next-) CC's are set as by ldhi. **ATTENTION!:** (a) Previous instr. MUST have its SCC-bit OFF; (b) IMM-bit MUST be OFF, rs2 MUST be r0 (to prevent int-forw.). Otherwise rd:=garbage!! **NOTES:** (a) see fig. A.1.1 for PSW; (b) rs1 is discarded.
putpsw:	(1) PSW := [rs1 + shortSOURCE2]<12:0> . **ATTENTION!:** (a) the SCC-bit MUST be OFF; (b) the following instruction must NOT be: callx, callr, calli, ret, reti (i.e. NOT modify CWP), and must NOT set the CC's. (c) new PSW is NOT in effect during the first cycle following execution of this instr. **NOTES:** (a) see fig. A.1.1 for PSW; (b) rd is discarded.
calli	(1) CWP := CWP-1 modulo 8 (change window like call). (2) rd := LSTPC ; CC's possibly affected; like getlpc. **NOTES:** (a) LSTPC is saved into rd of the NEW window; (b) the rs1, shortSOURCE2 fields are discarded; (c) if interrupts are enabled, an overflow trap may occur, like for call instructions. (d) this instr. is intended for use only by the H/W interrupt mech. (fig.A.5.1) -- NOT by S/W.

A.5   Interrupts and Traps

Figure A.5.1 describes the automatic hardware actions which occur on interrupts and traps and the possible causes and respective priorities of interrupts/traps. The overall effect of an interrupt/trap is that it transfers control to the interrupt-handler, as if the interrupted instruction had never even started executing. (The only exception is an external interrupt not due to a page-fault during a memory-write cycle; see below.) Also, the interrupt/trap mechanism saves enough information, so that later the normal-user visible state can be reconstructed and the interrupted instruction can be restarted.

When an interrupt/trap occurs, the normal-user visible state (§ A.1) is protected from being altered by the executing instruction. The only exception is that a memory-write access in progress is allowed to complete if it can do so. This is possible if the interrupt was *not* due to a page-fault caused by that access. Furthermore, if execution has proceeded so far that write access has been started, no further trap (that is anomaly originating from the CPU) can occur during the execution of that instruction, since all traps occur during the address calculation cycle for load and store instructions. In other words, the only possible cause for the abortion of this instruction might have been an external *non-page-fault* interrupt. Therefore, if the memory-write access was allowed to complete, it must have been a *correct* access. When the same instruction is restarted later, after the interrupt-handling routine returns, it will repeat the same write-access, and the overall result will be the same as if the instruction had executed only once.

While most of the normal-user visible state is protected from being altered by the executing instruction, there are some parts of it that must be altered before the interrupt-handler can start executing. Those parts, then, must either be altered in a known and *reversible* manner, or their previous value must be saved before it is altered. When returning from the interrupt, the alterations must be reversed and the saved values restored.

The state which is altered in a reversible way is the PSW I bit and the CWP. The I bit was ON since the interrupt/trap occurred; and it is turned OFF. The CWP is decremented by the hardwired calli instruction. This decrementation will always occur, since the calli executes with interrupts disabled. Both of these changes are reversed by the reti instruction. Note that the I bit is not necessarily

Figure A.5.1:   Interrupts and Traps in RISC II.

Situation:	Activities, Effects, Notes:
Interrupt or Trap occurs:	**INTRODUCTORY NOTES:** (1) Interrupts (i.e. external) and Traps (i.e. internal) are sampled/detected near the "middle" of every cycle; (2) Instructions "commit", i.e. modify the user-visible state of the CPU (fig. A.1.1), near the end of their "Execute" cycle. **AUTOMATIC (HARDWIRED) ACTIVITIES AND EFFECTS:** Assume the Interrupt/Trap occurs during cycle#i. (1) The instruction executing during cycle#i is ABORTED, i.e. it is NOT allowed to "commit" -- Except that: (i) the PC's operate independently, and (ii) a memory-write that may have started will be allowed to complete (if it may). (2) The instruction that has been fetched during cycle#i (or i-1) is DISCARDED, and replaced by the (hardwired) instr.: **calli, SCC-OFF, rd=25, rs1-shortSOURCE2=garbage.** (3) The PSW (fig. A.1.1) is modified as follows: I:=OFF (disable interrupts); P:=S ; S:=ON (system-mode). (4) Instruction-Fetching starts at the address specified by the Interrupt-Vector, and NXTPC is loaded with that value. **INTERRUPT CAUSES, AND CORRESPONDING VECTORS:** (1) Reset-pin pulsed high; Vector=80000000 Hexadecimal. (2) Interrupt-Request-Pin pulsed high; Vector=80000010 Hexad. **TRAP CAUSES, AND CORRESPONDING VECTORS:** (1) Illegal opcode (fig. A.4.2) executed; Vect=80000000 Hexad. (2) Priviledged opcode (fig. A.4.2) executed while S==OFF (i.e. in user-mode); Vector=80000000 Hexadecimal. (3) Address-Misalignment (fig. A.4.4-5); Vect=80000000 Hexad. (4) Reg-File Overflow (fig. A.4.6(call)); Vect=80000020 Hexad. (5) Reg-File Underflow (fig. A.4.6(ret)); Vect=80000030 Hexad. **INTERRUPT/TRAP DISABLING:** All interrupts and traps, except the one caused by the Reset-pin, are disabled whenever the I bit of PSW is OFF. **PRIORITIES:** In case more than one interrupt/trap causes are present at once, the Vector is determined according to the priority: 80000000 has highest priority, 80000020 and 80000030 have medium priority (they cannot occur simultaneously), and 80000010 has lowest priority. **NOTES:** (1) In cycle#(i+1), the hardwired calli instruction will execute, changing the window, and saving LSTPC into reg. 25 of the new window. The value saved is equal to the PC of cycle#i. (2) In cycle#(i+1), the instr. @ Vector will be fetched, and it will execute in cycle#(i+2). That instruction must be a getlpc, to save LSTPC of cycle#(i+2) = NXTPC of cycle#i.

ON when a reset occurs; however, when a reset is used we don't care to save the previous state.

The part of the state that is saved before it is altered consists of the PSW S bit, the NXTPC, and the PC. The S bit is saved into the P bit by automatic hardwired action, and it is restored by the reti instruction. The PC is saved into LSTPC, which is subsequently saved into register 25 of the new window by the calli instruction. The NXTPC goes into PC, which then goes into LSTPC, and which must be saved by the first instruction of the interrupt-handler. That instruction *must* be a getlpc, and it will place this value typically into register 24. After the completion of the interrupt-handling, these two values must be restored in the following fashion:

$$\text{jmpx (alw), r25} + 0 \text{ ;}$$
$$\text{reti (alw), r24} + 0 \text{ .}$$

Notice that the detection of register-window overflows works in such a way that registers 25 through 16 (the locals) of the window just below the current one, are guaranteed to be free whenever interrupts are enabled, provided this condition held true when interrupts were originally enabled (§ 3.2.2). The *calli* and *getlpc* instructions save LSTPC into two of those local registers on interrupts. The interrupt-handler may also use those local registers (and only those) as scratch memory.

While the normal-user visible state is saved on an interrupt/trap, the i-h programmer visible state (§ A.1) is *not* saved. This means that interrupts/traps must NOT nest without prior appropriate arrangements. Thus, before the interrupt-handler re-enables interrupts, or modifies the CC's, or uses any registers other than 25 through 16, or calls a subroutine, it *must* save PSW somewhere (e.g. getpsw r23, r0, r0), and make sure that there are more free windows below the current one. As the last step before returning from the interrupt-handler with the instruction-pair *jmpx – reti*, the PSW must be restored (e.g. putpsw r0, r23, r0). This restores the environment and the state that existed before this interrupt occurred.

Bibliography

[AhUl77]   A. Aho, J. Ullman: "Principles of Compiler Design", Addison-Wesley Publishing Co, 1977.

[AlWo75]   G. Alexander, D. Wortman: "Static and Dynamic characteristics of XPL programs", IEEE Computer magazine, Nov. 1975, pp.41-46.

[ArOu82]   M. Arnold, J. Ousterhout: "Lyra: A New Approach to Geometric Layout Rule Checking", 19th Design Automation Conf. Proceedings, ACM-IEEE, June 1982.

[BaMa78]   Barbacci, Mario, e.a.: "The ISPS Computer Description Language", Carnegie-Mellon University, 1978.

[Bask78]   Baskett F.: "A VLSI Pascal machine", Public Lecture, U.C.Berkeley, Fall 78.

[Beye81]   J. Beyers, L. Dohse, J. Fucetola, R. Kochis, C. Lob, G. Taylor, E. Zeller: "A 32-Bit VLSI CPU Chip," IEEE JSSC, vol. SC-16, no.5, pp. 537-542, October 1981.

[Blom83]   R. Blomseth: "A Big RISC", Report No. UCB/CSD 83/143, Computer Sci. Div., EECS, Univ. of California, Berkeley, CA 94720, November 1983.

[Camp80]   R. Campbell: "Compiling C for the Reduced Instruction Set Computer", Master's report, EECS, U. C. Berkeley 94720, December

202

1980.

[ClGr77]   D. Clark, C. Green: "An Empirical Study of List Structure in Lisp", Communications of the ACM, Vol.20, No.2, pp.78-87, Feb. 1977.

[Cock83]   J. Cocke: Informal discussion on the IBM 801 mini-computer, U.C.Berkeley Campus, June 1983.

[Corc80]   G. Corcoran: "Using ISPS to Specify the RISC I Architecture and Implementation", Master's report, EECS, U. C. Berkeley 94720, December 1980.

[DEC81]   Digital Equipment Co.: "VAX Hardware Handbook": System Throughput Considerations, Appendix K, p. 532 in 1980-81 edition.

[DiML82]   D. Ditzel, H. McLellan: "Register Allocation for Free: The C Machine Stack Cache", Proceedings, Symp. on Architectural Support for Progr. Lang. and Oper. Systems, Palo Alto, Ca, March 1982, (ACM: SIGARCH CAN vol. 10 no. 2, SIGPLAN Notices vol. 17 no. 4), pp. 48-56.

[DiPa80]   D. Ditzel, D. Patterson: "Retrospective on High-Level Language Computer Architecture", Proc. of the 7th Annual Symposium on Computer Architecture, ACM SIGARCH 8.3, pp. 97-104, May 1980.

[EiWi77]   E. Eichelberger, T. Williams: "A logic design structure for LSI testability", Proceedings, 14th Design Automation Conference, pp.462-468, ACM, New York, June 1977; also in J. Des. Autom. Fault-Tolerant Comp., 2.2, pp.165-178, May 1978.

[Elsh76]   J. Elshoff: "A Numerical Profile of Commercial PL/I Programs", Software - Practice and Experience, vol.6, 1976, pp.505-525.

[Fitz81]   D. Fitzpatrick, J. Foderaro, M. Katevenis, H. Landman, D. Patter-
           son, J. Peek, Z. Peshkess, C. Séquin, R. Sherburne, K. VanDyke:
           "VLSI Implementations of a Reduced Instruction Set Computer",
           VLSI Systems and Computations, Carnegie-Mellon Univ. Confer-
           ence, Computer Science Press, pp. 327-336, October 1981. Also in:
           "A RISCy Approach to VLSI", VLSI Design, vol. II, no. 4, pp.
           14-20, 4th qu. 1981; and in: Computer Architecture News (ACM
           SIGARCH), vol. 10, no. 1, pp. 28-32, March 1982.

[FitzME]   D. Fitzpatrick: *Mextra:* a Manhattan circuit extraction program, U.
           C. Berkeley. See e.g. "1983 VLSI Tools -- Selected works by the
           original artists", report No. UCB/CSD-83/115, Comp. Sci. Div., U.
           C. Berkeley, CA 94720, March 1983.

[FoVP82]   J. Foderaro, K. VanDyke, D. Patterson: "Running RISCs", VLSI
           Design, vol. III, no. 5, pp. 27-32, Sep/Oct. 1982.

[FrSp81]   E. Frank, R. Sproull: "Testing and Debugging Custom Integrated
           Circuits", ACM Computing Surveys, Vol.13 #4, pp.425-451,
           December 1981.

[Fuji83]   R. Fujimoto: "VLSI Communication Components for Multicomputer
           Networks", Doctoral Dissertation, EECS, Univ. of Calif., Berkeley
           94720, August 1983.

[GaVD81]   P. Garrison, K. VanDyke: "Compact RISC", CS292R Final Class
           Report, Comp. Sci., U.C.Berkeley 94720, December 1981.

[HaKe80]   D. Halbert, P. Kessler: "Windows of Overlapping Register
           Frames", CS292R-course final report, Univ. of California, Berke-
           ley, June 1980.

[Henn82]   J. Hennessy, N. Jouppi, F. Baskett, T. Gross, J. Gill:
           "Hardware/Software Tradeoffs for Increased Performance",

204

Proceedings, Symp. on Architectural Support for Programming Languages and Operating Systems, March 82, ACM SIGARCH-CAN-10.2 SIGPLAN-17.4, pp. 2-11.

[Henn83]   J. Hennessy, N. Jouppi, S. Przybylski, C. Rowen, T. Gross: "Design of a High Performance VLSI Processor", Proceedings, 3rd Caltech Conference on VLSI, Pasadena, CA, March 83, Ed. R.Bryant, Comp. Sci. Press, pp. 33-54.

[Kate80]   M. Katevenis: "A Proposal for the LSI Implementation of the RISC I CPU (using a 3-phase clock)", Internal U.C.Berkeley Working Paper, 23 pages, September 1980.

[Kess82]   P. Kessler: private communication, U.C.Berkeley, August 1982.

[Knut71]   D. Knuth: "An Empirical Study of FORTRAN Programs", Software - Practice and Experience, vol. 1, 1971, pp.105-133.

[Liou83]   D. Lioupis: "The RISC II Computer", Internal U.C.Berkeley Working Paper, 25 pages, June 1983.

[Lund77]   A. Lunde: "Empirical Evaluation of some Features of Instruction Set Processor Architectures", Communications of the ACM, 20.3, March 77, pp.143-153.

[Miro82]   J. Miros: "A C Compiler for RISC I", Master's report, EECS, U. C. Berkeley 94720, August 1982.

[NaPe73]   L. W. Nagel, D. O. Pederson: "Simulation program with integrated circuit emphasis", Proc. 16th Midwest Symp. Circ. Theory, (Waterloo, Canada), Apr. 1973.
L. W. Nagel: "SPICE2: A computer program to simulate semiconductor circuits", ERL Memo ERL-M520, Univ. of California, Berkeley, May 1975.

[Orga82]   E. Organick: "A Programmer's View of the Intel 432 System",
            McGraw-Hill, Hightstown, N.J., 1982.

[Oust81]   J. Ousterhout: "Caesar: An Interactive Editor for VLSI Circuits",
            VLSI Design II(4), Nov. 81, pp. 34-38.

[Oust83]   J. Ousterhout: "Crystal: A Timing Analyzer for NMOS VLSI Cir-
            cuits", Proceedings of the 3rd Caltech Conference on VLSI, March
            1983.

[PaDi80]   D. Patterson, D. Ditzel: "The Case for the Reduced Instruction Set
            Computer", Computer Architecture News, ACM SIGARCH, 8.6,
            Oct. 1980, pp.25-33.

[PaPi82]   D. Patterson, R. Piepho: "RISC Assessment: A High-Level
            Language Experiment", Proc. of the 9th Annual Symposium on
            Computer Architecture, ACM SIGARCH 10.3, APR. 1982, pp. 3-8;
            Also in: "Assessing RISCs in HLL Support", IEEE Micro Maga-
            zine, Vol. 2, No. 4, NOV. 1982, pp. 9-19.

[PaSe81]   D. Patterson, C. Séquin: "RISC I: A Reduced Instruction Set VLSI
            Computer", Proc. of the 8th Symposium on Computer Architecture,
            ACM SIGARCH CAN 9.3, pp. 443-457, May 1981.

[PaSe82]   D. Patterson, C. Séquin: "A VLSI RISC", IEEE Computer Maga-
            zine, vol.15, no.9, Sept. 1982, pp. 8-21; also available from
            U.C.Berkeley, E.R.L., as Memo. UCB/ERL M82/10, Feb. 1982.

[Patt83]   D. Patterson, P. Garrison, M. Hill, D. Lioupis, C. Nyberg, T. Sip-
            pel, K. VanDyke: "Architecture of a VLSI Instruction Cache",
            Proc. of the 10th Symposium on Computer Architecture, ACM
            SIGARCH CAN 11.3, pp. 108-116, June 1983.

206

[PeSh77]   B. Peuto, L. Shustek: "An Instruction Timing Model of CPU Performance", Proc. of the 4th Symposium on Computer Architecture, ACM, IEEE, March 1977.

[Radi82]   G. Radin: "The 801 Minicomputer", Proceedings, Symp. on Architectural Support for Programming Languages and Operating Systems, March 82, ACM SIGARCH-CAN-10.2 SIGPLAN-17.4, pp. 39,47.

[SKPS82]   R. Sherburne, M. Katevenis, D. Patterson, C. Séquin: "Datapath Design for RISC", Proceedings, Conference on Advanced Research in VLSI, M.I.T., Jan. 1982, pp. 53-62.

[Sher84]   R. Sherburne: "Processor Design Tradeoffs in VLSI", Doctoral Dissertation, 1984. Available as Report No. UCB/CSD 84/173, Computer Science Div., EECS, University of California, Berkeley, CA 94720.

[Shus78]   L. Shustek: "Analysis and Performance of Computer Instruction Sets", Doctoral Dissertation, Stanford University, 1977 or 78.

[Site79]   Sites R. L.: "How to use 1000 registers", Proc. Caltech Conference on VLSI, Jan. 1979, pp. 527-532.

[Smit82]   A. Smith: "Cache Memories", ACM Computing Surveys, Vol.14, No.3, pp.473-530, Sept. 1982.

[Stre78]   W. Strecker: "VAX-11/780: A Virtual Address Extension to the DEC PDP-11 Family", AFIPS Conf. Proc., Vol. 47, 1978 NCC, pp.967-980.

[TaSe83]   Y. Tamir, C. Séquin: "Strategies for Managing the Register File in RISC", IEEE Transactions on Computers, vol. C-32, no. 11, November 1983, pp. 977-989.

[Tami81]   Y. Tamir: "Simulation and Performance Evaluation of the RISC Architecture", Electronics Research Lab. Memo. UCB/ERL M81/17, Univ. of California, Berkeley, CA 94720, March 1981.

[Tane78]   A. Tanenbaum: "Implications of Structured Programming for Machine Architecture", Communications of the ACM, 21.3, March 78, pp.237-246.

[TermES]   C. Terman: *Esim:* a switch-level simulation program, Massachusetts Institute of Technology.

[Thor64]   J. Thornton: "Parallel operation in the Control Data 6600", AFIPS Proc. FJCC, pt.2 vol.26, pp.33-40. 1964. Also in: Bell, Newell: "Computer Structures: Readings and Examples", McGraw Hill Book Co., 1971, pp.489-496.

[Tyne81]   P. Tyner: "iAPX-432 General Data Processor Architecture Reference Manual", Order #171860-001, Intel, Santa Clara, Calif., 1981.

[Utle78]   B. Utley e.a.: "IBM System/38 Technical Developments", IBM GS80-0237, 1978.

[VDFo82]   K. VanDyke, J. Foderaro: "SLANG: A Logic Simulation Language", Research Project (Master's Report), CS, U.C.Berkeley, June 1982.

[WeinLC]   P. Weinberger, *Lcomp*: a compiler for profiling, Bell Laboratories, Murray Hill.

[WiAn73]   M. Williams, J. Angell: "Enhancing testability of LSI circuits via test points and additional logic", IEEE Trans. on Computers, C-22.1, pp.46-60, January 1973.

Index

A

addressing modes of RISC I & II, 45-47, 70-74

architecture of RISC I & II, 43-63, 177-199

area (of silicon, in RISC II), 116

assembly vs. compiled, 53, 77-78

B

banks of registers (multiple), 52-63, 132-144

Berkeley RISC project, 5

branch, delayed, 47-49

   -target address, 152-154

by-passing (internal forwarding), 66, 111

C

caches vs. windows (of registers), 132-136

CAD programs, critical loops of, 36-40

catch instruction, 140

chaining (internal forwarding), 66, 111

chronology of the Berkeley RISC project, 6

circular window organization, 56-58

clock phases, 101-104

CMOS RISC II, 7

compactness of code, 78-81

compare-and-branch schemes, 150-151

comparisons for fast-branch, 156-158

compiled vs. assembly, 53, 77-78

complexity vs. size vs. speed, 2

concept of RISC, 1

conceptual window stack, 59-62

R

S